The reprinting of this book is due to many people who thought it was too important a resource to be out of print and to the countless people who still request copies of the book even though it has not been available for almost two years.

In getting *Kansas City Style* reprinted the authors want to acknowledge the efforts of Dale Chaffin, Chief Operating Officer of Shook, Hardy and Bacon and the support given by Robert L. Collins, Director of Kansas City, Missouri's Planning And Development Department and Lisa Lassman Briscoe, Administrator of the Landmarks Commission of Kansas City, Missouri.

Kansas City Style
A social and cultural history of Kansas City
as seen through its lost architecture.

Third printing: September, 1992
© 1992 Dory DeAngelo and Jane Fifield Flynn
Fifield Publishing Co.

ISBN Number: 0-9633758-1-4
Library of Congress Catalog Card Number: 92-073620

Printed in the United States of America

Dory DeAngelo

KANSAS CITY STYLE

A social and cultural history of Kansas City
as seen through its lost architecture

The law offices of

SHOOK, HARDY & BACON

present

A social and cultural
history of Kansas City
as seen through its
lost architecture

by

Dory DeAngelo
Jane Fifield Flynn

Editor

Rosanne Wickman

Fifield Publishing Company

P.O. Box 30302
Kansas City, Missouri 64112

CONTENTS

A CONTINUITY OF EXCELLENCE — Key figures in the evolution of the firm that eventually became Shook, Hardy & Bacon include (top to bottom) Frank P. Sebree I (1854 - 1940), Edgar Shook (1894 - 1970) , David R. Hardy (1917 - 1976); and Charles L. Bacon (1909 - 1989), the latter remembered as one of the firm's most beloved personalities. Bacon is shown seated in the thirtieth-floor foyer of the firm's offices in One Kansas City Place.
(Bacon photo: Mariann Kilroy)

SHOOK, HARDY & BACON
BEGINS A SECOND CENTURY
OF GROWTH

Law firm has been witness and partner in
significant Kansas City history.

W hen a building vanishes from the landscape, it is simply gone. The impact of a brilliant lawyer may beneficially influence his successors for years to come.

A testimony to this truth is the ever-enlarging success of the law firm of Shook, Hardy & Bacon. In 1889 when Frank P. Sebree moved from Marshall, Missouri, to Kansas City and hung out his shingle (with partner William A. Alderson), he could not know that he was laying the foundation of what was to become, within a century, the city's largest law firm.

Commencing its second century in 1990, Shook, Hardy & Bacon has seen many of the buildings in this volume rise and fall during its lifetime. None of the principal structures pictured in this book exists today, living on only in memory and in a few specialized archives. In contrast, the law firm's contributions over its first 100 years have had an enduring impact on our community's legal history.

Sebree proved to be the cornerstone whose personal and professional integrity formed his law firm's operations. From the outset, Sebree demonstrated his belief that community involvement was integral to his activities as an attorney. Chairman of the Jackson County Democratic Committee in 1897, the next year he ran (unsuccessfully) for Mayor of Kansas City, but in short order was appointed by Gov. Lon Stephens to the 1899 Anti-Trust Convention in Chicago. Active in both the Missouri and American Bar Associations, he subsequently served on the Board of Police Commissioners as well as the Jackson County Election Board and the Kansas City Park Board.

During this time, the firm's name evolved through several formations: McDougal & Sebree; Sebree, Conrad and Wendorff and — when son Samuel Boyd joined the firm in 1920 — Sebree & Sebree. Over the next few years, the firm was strengthened with the additions of partners including John Wendorff, Henry Lee Jost and Robert Edgar Shook.

Born in Nevada, Missouri, the son of a minister, Shook served in the Army during World War I, then entered law school at the University of Missouri - Columbia. After practicing law briefly in Marshall, Missouri, he came to Kansas City. In 1934 he joined the Sebrees and the firm became Sebree, Sebree & Shook.

During the 1930s, it was Shook who spoke most loudly against Kansas City's crooked Pendergast machine before that became popular. In 1939, Shook was named "Man of the Year" by the Metro Club. When, in the wake of the Pendergast revelations, the Missouri legislature put the Kansas City Police Department under state control, Shook was named chairman of the newly created Police Board.

The next year, which brought the death of Frank P. Sebree, lawyers George Gisler and David R. Hardy joined the offices.

Ultimately it was Hardy who, following service in World War II, was instrumental in guiding the firm to steady growth. His keen legal talent and amazing trial ability moved the firm toward more litigation. Hardy's greatest achievements came as a trial lawyer in the field of products liability, libel law and antitrust matters. Upon his death in 1976 at age 59, the Kansas City Star called him "the ultimate, the consummate trial lawyer."

A further strengthening of Shook, Hardy & Bacon's foundation came in 1957 when Charles L. Bacon, formerly general counsel for Skelly Oil Co., joined the firm. Like Hardy, he embodied a keen legal talent that was matched by his commitment to community service. Bacon, like Frank P. Sebree I, a product of Marshall, Missouri, moved to Kansas City after distinguished service in World War II. Active in the American Legion, he was elected its National Commander in 1962. Bacon served from 1951-54 on the governor's special education commission, then later

as state chairman for Stuart Symington's 1958 and 1964 senatorial campaigns. In the 1970s, Bacon helped bring about the restoration of the Liberty Memorial and was instrumental in finding a full-time curator for its World War I Museum. Capping these achievements, he was elected in 1970 to the prestigious Academy of Missouri Squires, an organization of 100 living Missourians who represent ideas of service and commitment to American democratic principles.

By 1957, Frank P. Sebree II, was carrying on the community service tradition of his grandfather, Frank P. Sebree I. He served two terms on the Kansas City, Missouri Council; was chairman of the Citizens Association in 1961-62; and for twelve years served as President and/or Chairman of the Truman Medical Center Board of Directors.

Shook, Hardy & Bacon's headquarter offices occupy ten floors of One Kansas City Place at 1200 Main Street in downtown Kansas City, Mo. (Architecural Fotografics)

The 1950s proved to be a watershed decade for Shook, Hardy & Bacon with a number of cases securing its reputation as a leader in handling products liability cases. After Hardy won what was then the largest plaintiff's verdict ever awarded in Missouri (Moore vs. Ready Mixed Concrete Co,) the firm's defense work accelerated markedly. He went on to successfully defend Philip Morris in a landmark case claiming personal injuries due to smoking. Continued successes led to the firm's present national prominence in defense of pharmaceutical and medical device products liability litigation.

By 1967, a slow but steady growth had brought the firm's complement to 21 lawyers and 17 support staff members. In 1973 the firm took on its present name — Shook, Hardy & Bacon — and proceeded to set a new, unmatched pace for growth in the decade to follow. A Washington, D.C., office was opened in 1975, by which time the firm was nationally recognized for its work in the fields of general civil and trial practice, products liability, anti-trust litigation, business and corporate, insurance, probate, taxation, estate planning, real estate and administrative law.

By 1982, the Kansas City Business Journal listed Shook, Hardy & Bacon as the city's second largest law firm. Attorneys and support staff totaled 160 persons. During the period of 1985-89, the firm more than doubled its size and was coming up to speed technologically with the enlargement and sophistication of its automation and computer systems — all necessary to the handling of large numbers of complex legal matters.

One of the most graceful features in the headquarters offices of Shook, Hardy & Bacon is this spiral staircase that connects the thirtieth and thirty-first floors. It was designed by PBNI Architects, Inc. (Architectural Fotografics)

Today, the firm's lawyers are aided by over 100 research analysts and legal assistants, and supported by a 30,000-volume law library, computerized document storage, in-house publishing capabilities and computerized lists of experts in various disciplines.

Shook, Hardy & Bacon has brought its legal expertise to bear in structuring and closing venture capital transactions on behalf of both investors and emerging companies. For major clients, they have handled acquisitions, leveraged buyouts, recapitalizations, shareholders rights plans and more. Recently, the firm handled the Marion Merrell Dow Inc. merger and acquisition transaction. This was the fourth largest transaction of its type conducted in the United States during 1989. The firm's most recent expansion has come with the addition of an Environmental Law Section and the development of a sophisticated international law practice extending the firm's legal work around the globe.

In 1982, the firm expanded its regional presence by opening an office in the Corporate Woods Complex in Overland Park. With Shook, Hardy & Bacon's reputation for solid, quality work, the Kansas office quickly claimed its place in the top ten largest firms in Kansas. In 1989, the firm opened a London office. But Metropolitan Kansas City is still the heart of the firm with the downtown Kansas City, Missouri offices located on ten floors of the One Kansas City Place building.

Recent law school graduates and seasoned lawyers alike seek out Shook, Hardy & Bacon as a place for sound professional growth. And who are these talented individuals who ultimately qualify for a spot on the Shook, Hardy & Bacon roster? Of course, they possess first-rate legal minds, but they also are exceptional personalities who are stimulated by the chance to work with outstanding peers and an extraordinary client base. Many supplement their day-to-day work with pro bono cases such as the firm's recent argument before the Supreme Court of the United States on the right to die issue, and almost all will become involved with community improvement and philanthropic work. Another manifestation of that community commitment is the SHB Volunteer Corps, which organizes and staffs charitable events in the community.

Each SHB lawyer is committed to the notion that there is no such thing as a "routine" legal issue, that every client deserves the highest order of professional attention. Out of the representation of some of these clients will come landmark actions that may contribute to precedent and forever change a legal principle affecting all citizens.

As this remarkable law firm embarks on its second century, it can proceed with its mission secure in the knowledge its efforts are based on generations of excellence. In that same way that the buildings depicted in this volume shaped and influenced the lives of their inhabitants, Shook, Hardy & Bacon will continue to make its philosophy of beneficial service felt for years to come.

David S. Hudson

(This article is based on historical information provided by Mickie Denison, Fred L. Lee, Karen Johnson, Michael Rutledge and Christine Hughes.)

The Kansas offices of Shook, Hardy & Bacon are located in this handsome building in the Corporate Woods office park in Johnson County
(Architectural Fotografics)

SHOOK, HARDY & BACON
ATTORNEYS

PARTNERS
Lane D. Bauer
Frank P. Sebree II
Frederick Beihl
William W. Shinn
John C. Dods
Donald K. Hoel
William K. Waugh, Jr.
Lee E. Stanford
David K. Hardy
William G. Zimmerman
Robert E. Northrip
Patrick McLarney
Harvey L. Kaplan
John C. Monica
Sam L. Colville
Gene E. Voigts
James T. Newsom#
Leo P. Dreyer
Elwood L. Thomas
Stephen D. Aliber
Patrick M. Sirridge
Larry R. O'Neal
Laurel J. Harbour
Allen R. Purvis
Richard D. Woods
Bernard V. O'Neill, Jr.
Gary R. Long
Timothy A. Pratt

Gary L. Whittier
Jennings J. Newcom
Vivian W. McLeod
J. Eugene Balloun*
Ron Bodinson*
Dennis R. Dow
Richard E. McLeod
Peter E. Strand
John F. Murphy
Laura D. Stith
Andrew See
J. Scott McCandless
Robert D. Grossman*
J. Richard Golub*
Marie S. Woodbury
John S. Johnston
Thomas R. Buchanan*
Judith L. Hancock
David J. Waxse*
Stanley P. Weiner
C. Maxwell Logan*
Alson R. Martin*
Walter L. Cofer
Richard M. Wright, Jr.
Rhonda E. Fawcett
Stephen E. Scheve
James M. Ash
Jeffrey S. Nelson*
Kip A.Wiggins

Nancy Schmidt Roush*
Kevin R. Sweeney
Clyde W. Curtis
Anthony J. Andrade#
William E. Sampson*
Robert J. Janowitz
William H. Colby
Michael L. Koon
Gary D. Gilson
Barkley Clark
Leanne DeShong

OF COUNSEL
Elinor P. Schroeder*
David M. Claycomb
Mary Beth Blake*
James C. Neet, Jr.
Sylvan Siegler

RETIRED
David H. Clark

STAFF ATTORNEYS
Judith A. Hollinger
Karen I. Johnson
Grace L. Spezia
Mindy J. Morse
Lori Burns-Bucklew

ASSOCIATES
David M. Peterson
Eugene S. Peck
Matthew D. Keenan*
Joseph M. Rebein
Gary B. Brewer
Robert K. Kirkland
David W. Brooks
Jeffrey A. Burns
Roger C. Geary
William J. Crampton
Timothy M. O'Brien*
Lisa White Hardwick
Gregory L. Fowler
James A. Wilson
Michel R. Mangrum
SueAnn S. Wright
Craig A. Hunt
Emily G. Cena
George E. Wolf III
Sandra L. Thomas
Candis Young
Judith S. Barber
Anne Stohr O'Brien*
Larry M. Schumaker
Joseph S. Gall
William S. Ohlemeyer
Donald J. Kemna

Richard H. Page*
Shannon L. Spangler
Craig E. Gustafson
John T. Steere*
Daniel R. Ray*
Martha S. Warren
Barbara A. Harmon*
Robert T. Adams
Scott W. Sayler
Mark Moedritzer
Jamie M. Clark*
Karen C. Warner
Cyprienne Simchowitz
W. Edward Reeves
Randy J. Carter
William L. Allinder
Margaret D. Lineberry
Steven R. Koch
John W. Simpson
Kevin J. Driscoll
Daniel W. Shinn
Shari L. Wright
Richard L. Becker
Wanda M. Temm*
Todd W. Ruskamp
Randall E. Pratt
Denise M. Freeman
Curtis G. Oltmans
C. Sue Love

Victoria L. Ruhga
Lori C. McGroder
Cynthia M. Harrington*
David H. Reinmiller
Jeffrey R. Berg
Merry Evans
Kelly W. Schemenauer
Denise M. Oas
Daryl J. Douglas
James P. Hostetter
James W. Stubblefield
Robert J. McCully
Christopher M. McDonald
Michael G. Deal
Kenneth E. Nelson
G. David Porter
Peter G. Edwards
Madeleine M. McDonough

*= Kansas Office
#= London Office

SHOOK, HARDY & BACON'S
NAME AND BUILDING CHRONOLOGY

(As of September 5, 1990)

1889-90 Alderson & Sebree
Long Brothers Office Building
515 Main

1891 Buckner & Sebree
New York Life Building
20 W. 9th Street

1892-02 McDougal & Sebree
New York Life Building
20 E. 9th Street

1903-04 Frank P. Sebree
New York Life Building
20 W. 9th Street

1905-06 Frank P. Sebree
New England Building
112 W. 9th Street

1907 Frank P. Sebree
Scarritt Building
818 Grand

1908-17 Sebree, Conrad & Wendorff
Scarritt Building
818 Grand

1918-19 Sebree, Conrad & Sebrree
Scarritt Building
818 Grand

1920-22 Sebree & Sebree
Scarritt Building
818 Grand

1923-33 Sebree, Jost & Sebree
Commerce Building
922 Walnut

1934-37 Sebree, Sebree & Shook
Commerce Building
922 Walnut

1938-40 Sebree, Sebree & Shook
Federal Reserve Building
925 Grand

1941-46 Sebree, Shook & Gisler
Federal Reserve Building
925 Grand

1947-55 Sebree, Shook, Hardy & Hunter
Federal Reserve Building
925 Grand

1956-61 Sebree, Shook, Hardy & Ottman
Benton Building
915 Grand

1962-71 Shook, Hardy, Ottman, Mitchell & Bacon
Benton Building
915 Grand

1972-73 Shook, Hardy, Mitchell & Bacon
Benton Building
915 Grand

1973-75 Shook, Hardy & Bacon
Benton Building
915 Grand

1976-88 Shook, Hardy & Bacon
Mercantile Bank Tower Building
1101 Walnut Street

1982- Shook, Hardy & Bacon
Corporate Woods Building #40
9401 Indian Creek Pkwy.
Overland Park, Kansas

*1988- Shook, Hardy & Bacon
One Kansas City Place
1200 Main

*1989- Shook, Hardy & Bacon
19 Buckingham Gate
London, England

* Additional offices

FOREWORD

*T*he value of reading KANSAS CITY STYLE lies not just in learning the history of the architectural development of the city, nor in the memories awakened by the nostalgic illustrations, nor in exploring the fine craftsmanship evident in many of the buildings, but rather, the value of the book lies in the inherent lessons it provides for planning the future development and growth of Kansas City. We can do nothing about the past, but we can profitably learn from it.

The important question to be asked is why were so many fine buildings torn down? Like the buggy whip, many had become obsolete for their original use. Often the land under the structure became much more valuable when cleared, and so the building was razed. The inexorable growth of the city endangers older buildings as people and businesses spread out from the core city. If a building has a good location and can be economically restored for a germane use in that location, it has a chance of being saved. The Folly Theater is a case in point. It is Kansas City's only remaining turn-of-the-century theater of the thirteen that once graced downtown.

The most endangered buildings today are neighborhood schools and churches. A few have been successfully rehabilitated for community centers, but most are at risk unless an imaginative public can see their value as housing for the elderly or low income residents; both groups badly need housing.

Large buildings such as Kansas City's Union Station pose the most difficult problem for preservation. This magnificent building's survival will only be accomplished by the concerted will of the people of Kansas City. If everyone would read this book, KANSAS CITY STYLE, and learn the lessons it reveals, Union Station and the city's future planned growth would look much brighter.

Joan Dillon

Joan Kent Dillon, Board Member Emeritus of the National Trust for Historic Preservation, has been a central figure in Kansas City's historic preservation efforts for more than two decades. Perhaps most revered as "the lady who saved the Folly Theater," she has made her presence felt with such Kansas City cultural institutions as the Kansas City Art Institute, the Kansas City Arts Council, the Performing Arts Foundation (Folly Restoration Project), the Nelson-Atkins Museum of Art, Historic Kansas City, and the Kansas City Association of Trusts & Foundations. Nationally, she has given her time and talent to such organizations as the President's Committee on the Arts & Humanities, the League of Historic American Theaters, the American Arts Alliance and the Smithsonian Associates Board.

INTRODUCTION

Many people make pilgrimages to ruins of buildings in cities and towns across the world to see how past generations lived and worked. In many cities there are historic buildings that have been restored to give people the experience of what it was like to live in that space, in that period of time. There is nothing that reveals more vividly or accurately the history of a city than does its architecture, its built environment. Each building gives a visual record of the past, an identity, a place and a uniqueness that sets a city apart from other cities. Unfortunately, many buildings have been lost forever; no visual memory exists.

Kansas City's history, though short in the time line of world cities, began with the first log cabin built at the edge of the Missouri River over 170 years ago. Evidence of that log cabin, along with many of our early buildings, are gone. But through wisdom and forethought some photographs and records of early buildings have been saved.

In selecting what "lost" architecture was to be included in this book consideration was given to types of buildings, uses, design merit, and time periods. This book is an attempt to provide the reader with a sense of this city's structural envolution.

"Kansas City Style" is a celebration of our heritage, of the city's grandeur, and of its simple life. The buildings may be gone but through rare photographs and stories about the people who built them, and used them - our history lives on.

COVER — *Typical of the many small hosteleries that served Kansas City in the boom years of the 1890s was the quaint St. George Hotel at 922 Main Street, now the site of Boatmen's Center. The facade of the slim structure, designed in the Queen Anne style, was elegantly ornamented and featured two fantastical gargoyles with teeth bared in menacing grins.*
Kansas City, Missouri Public Library - Missouri Valley Special Collections.

TIVOLI GARDENS, 24th and Main streets. Built 1878; now site of the Westin Crown Center Hotel. Mary Keck

*T*ivoli Gardens was Kansas City's first amusement park, built in 1878 on the bluffs at 24th and Main streets that later became known as Signboard Hill.

In 1871, Henry Helmreich opened a brewery there to sell beer to Germans moving to nearby Dutch Hill (now the area surrounding the University of Missouri-Kansas City Medical School). The bluffs had many springs used in the brewing, and beer barrels were kept cool in caves around the hill. The brewery soon became a Sunday gathering place for the growing German population and Helmreich called it Bellevue Beer Garden (featuring LaFayette John's String Band).

Martin Keck, Helmreich's son-in-law, left Germany in 1855 and worked as a baker in Independence. He was a Santa Fe trader from 1862 until 1869, taking ox-drawn wagons loaded with goods to the West. He bought into the brewery, then in 1878 started Tivoli Gardens and built a home on the southwest corner of the property. One entrance to the gardens abutted the old Santa Fe Trail on Main Street. Another was a winding road at 24th Street.

Every Sunday Germans flocked to the six-acre gardens to drink beer, dance, hear concerts, bowl, stroll along landscaped walks, and take carriage rides.

In the 1870s, a "blue law" was passed prohibiting the sale of liquor and performances of concerts on Sundays. It sounded the death knell for Tivoli Gardens.

The development of Kansas City's cable car and street railway system had a lot to do with the growth of later amusement parks. Streetcar companies opened the

parks on their routes as a way to get more riders.

By the 1880s the city was still fairly concentrated between Third and 12th streets from Quality Hill to Troost Avenue. The parks usually were built "out in the country" at the end of the streetcar lines. The ride offered people a chance to get out of the city and have a good time at little cost — usually the price of carfare.

Troost Park was built by the Kansas City Railway Company at the end of its Troost Car Line. It covered six acres of land that originally was the Reverend James Porter farm. Attractions included a dance pavilion, a merry-go-round, a zoo, a boating lake and the famous "Shoot the Chutes" ride, the first thrill ride in the city. (Flat-bottomed boats moved up a sharply inclined track, then plunged into the lake to the delight of passengers.) The city purchased Troost Park's land in 1902 to include it in the municipal park system. The small lake still is visible from The Paseo.

Today the southwest corner of Independence and Hardesty avenues is paved over and crowded with fast-food restaurants.

TROOST AMUSEMENT PARK, 24th Street and Troost Avenue, built 1888. Kansas City, Missouri Public Library - Missouri Valley Special Collections

But in 1903 the Independence Avenue cable car left passengers there at the impressive entrance to the 10-acre Forest Park. Medieval towers and gardens invited people to enter the $195,000 park that Colonel John D. Hopkins, manager of Forest Park Highlands in St. Louis, had built. Attractions included a gallery of distorted mirrors and a scenic railway on which passengers sat in a train car as scenes of Europe, painted on canvas, rolled by. A Cave of the Winds swept audiences with "ocean breezes," and other attractions included a swimming pool, a mystery house, pony and donkey rides, a hall featuring vaudeville shows, and a dance pavilion. But the biggest attraction was a $15,000 carousel imported from England.

William Winner, president of the Kansas City Independence Railway, owned 2,400 acres of land in Independence. (His steam-driven car line was called "The Dummy Line," because the engines were covered with canvas to keep from frightening horses). Near what is now Truman Road and Interstate 435, Winner dammed Rock Creek, which ran through his property, and formed a 20-acre swimming and boating lake. The land became Mount Washington Park, one of the largest recreation areas in Missouri at the time. Many activities centered on the lake, including a ship anchored near the shore that served as a stage for plays and musical shows. A bandstand on an island featured performances by brass bands from around the country. Beyond these and other amusements, Mount Washington's natural beauty — wooded area, birds and wildlife — was a big attraction. The park closed in 1900, the lake was filled and landscaped and the site became the Mount Washington Cemetery.

Arthur E. Stillwell built Fairmount Park in 1897 to attract customers to his Air Line, the interurban railway from Second Street and Grand Avenue to Independence. The park, just north of what is now U. S. Highway 24, was an immediate success. An eight-acre lake had a two-story bathhouse and rental canoes and boats. The nine-hole Evanston Golf Club, a private club with 300 members next to the park, was a curiosity to the general public. Fairmount survived until 1933, when it was done in by a combination of the Depression and a fire that destroyed some of its facilities and polluted the lake.

Fairyland Amusement Park, built in 1923, survived fires, high winds, and lightning strikes, but was defeated by the opening of the World's of Fun theme park.

To those growing up between 1923 and the mid-1970s, Fairyland held fond memories. Many remember when their school's annual "Ditch Day" brought the whole student body to the park. And those who were children at the time recall saving their dimes and making their parents promise they could go once or twice during the summer months.

Fairyland was built on 80 acres of what then was farmland between 75th and 77th streets, from Prospect to Indiana avenues. It was reported to have cost one million dollars to build. It was served by the Prospect Avenue streetcar and later by trolley and motor bus, accessible by transfers from all over the area. There was plenty of parking for those who had cars.

From the moment visitors entered the gate, they were transported into a magical place. Clowns roamed the grounds and attractions included the Sky Rocket roller coaster, the roller-skating rink, fun houses, and a variety of rides including Ferris wheels, merry-go-rounds, a "Loop-the-Loop," electric bumper cars and pony rides. "The Chute" very like the earlier one at Troost Park, was one of the most popular rides. In the early days, the price for most rides was 10 cents. The Crystal Swimming Pool offered midnight dips.

Food was a big part of the Fairyland visits. Stands sold popcorn, cold drinks, ice cream, cotton candy, hotdogs and hamburgers. Picnic tables were on the grounds for those who brought their own lunch.

In the evenings, couples enjoyed the romantic open-air ballroom where such legendary swing bands as those of Count Basie, Glenn Miller and Cab Calloway played for moonlight dancing. The 80-by-300-foot ballroom cost $80,000 to build. Couples looked forward to the dance contests hoping to win the trophy for the best Charleston, bunny hug, fox trot and jitterbug.

Nature played havoc with Fairyland Park. In 1938, lightning destroyed The Chute and damaged the Sky Rocket; in 1941, a lightning fire destroyed a 100-foot-high curve of the repaired Rocket track. On a Sunday night in 1943, while couples at the pavilion were dancing to the music of Chauncey Downs and his Orchestra, a fire broke out and 10,000 people at the park were evacuated. The fire burned power lines and the surrounding residential area was plunged into darkness. Sixteen

concession stands were destroyed. Firefighters fought to contain the fire and keep it away from the Sky Rocket's wooden trestles. Each time there was a Fairyland fire it could be seen for miles; people flocked to see the sight. And children were said to have burst into tears, fearing they could never enjoy the park again.

Fairyland's owners were determined to keep it operating even after World's of Fun opened in 1973 north of the Missouri River. But in November of 1977, high winds caused extensive damage to the park and it was closed for good. In 1990, the old roller coaster track was sold to an amusement park in Oklahoma, and a Texas developer announced plans to build a residential complex on the property.

FAIRMOUNT AMUSEMENT PARK, U. S. Highway 24 at Northern Avenue opened in 1897; closed 1933. Now houses are on the site.
Jackson County Historical Society

ANDERSON SKELLY SERVICE STATION

*T*he first horseless carriage chugged noisily over Kansas City's streets and roads in the late 1880s. There were so few automobiles in 1896 that one was displayed as an oddity by the Barnum & Bailey Circus. But the industry grew quickly, and by the end of 1932, Americans had purchased about seven million automobiles. This created a huge market for gasoline and oil.

In 1911 one of the first filling stations — called "a motor car's watering trough" — operated curbside at 25th Street and Grand Avenue, serving as many as 60 autos in one day. The first drive-in filling station in the city was at 1725 Grand Avenue, and eventually this type of station replaced the curbside pumps. The city, perceiving danger in their proximity to traffic, ordered the curbside pumps removed in January 1928.

In the early 1930s, the Skelly Oil Company was one of the first large oil and gasoline producers to develop a major distribution center in Kansas City. Although its headquarters was in Tulsa, Oklahoma, the company maintained offices for many years at the southwest corner of 47th and Pennsylvania streets.

To capitalize on the heavy traffic along Pershing Road, the Anderson Skelly Service Station was built in 1934. It was designed by A. F. Larbers, the company's superintendent of equipment and construction.

The Art Deco style, cut-stone station was designed to harmonize with the appearance of the United States Post Office Building at 315 West Pershing Road (1933) and Union Station (1914).

Faltering sales forced the company to close the station. In 1979, while negotiations were under way to renovate the building as a drive-in banking facility, the building was demolished without a permit in the dead of night by the owners to create surface parking for 30 cars.

ANDERSON SKELLY SERVICE STATION
220 West Pershing Road.
Built 1934; demolished 1979.
Robert Noback, photographer

GARLAND BLOCK APARTMENTS,
Seventh Street and Woodland Avenue.
Woodland Elementary School's
playground is on the site today.
Kansas City, Missouri Public Library -
Missouri Valley Special Collections

KNICKERBOCKER APARTMENTS, 501-
525 Knickerbocker Place. Built 1910;
the north side apartments were
demolished in 1982.
Kansas City, Missouri Public Library -
Mission Valley Special Collections

FOUNTAIN PLACE, 1450
Independence Avenue. A car
dealership is on the site today.
Kansas City, Missouri Public Library -
Missouri Valley Special Collections

The 1880s were exciting times in Kansas City. The city's population, 124,474 in 1885, grew to almost 200,000 by 1899. There was a great real estate and building boom — $98 million was spent on new buildings from 1886 to 1889. The thriving business atmosphere created a large middle class that was not content to live in boarding houses but did not yet have the money to build homes.

Apartment living came to Kansas City in the mid-1880s. There had been tenement houses around the City Market area where families were packed into rooms stacked one on another. These meager dwellings were sometimes called "railroad flats" because the narrow buildings were built close to each other and had windows only at the front and back, leaving most tenants in the dark.

Fashionable apartment buildings for the well-to-do were a new idea. They originated in Paris, so they were called "French flats" in America. To distinguish them from the less desirable tenements, they were designed to resemble individual houses connected to each other. Some looked very much like castles or chateaus, and most were built in the best neighborhoods, allowing those who could not afford homes, addresses they needed to move up in society. The location of cable or streetcar lines had a lot to do with where the apartments were built — transportation to downtown jobs was important.

Apartments were built of brick or stone, and exteriors were busy with detail — spiral towers and gables. Most residents had their own entryways with carved decorations and porches with turned wood balustrades. Large chimneys running up the sides of the buildings allowed each unit to have at least one fireplace. Windows were important in those days before electricity became commonplace, so apartments had many bay windows and skylights to let in daylight.

Fountain Place, of Queen Anne design, took up a whole block on the north side of fashionable Independence Avenue between Lydia and Highland avenues. The Eastlake style Garland Block Apartments were just off Independence Avenue at Seventh Street and Woodland Avenue. The Queen Anne style Tullis Place on Quality Hill at Eighth and Jefferson streets, was a pair of buildings facing each other across a courtyard.

J. K. Landis built Landis Court a solid block of apartments between 17th and 18th streets, from Broadway to Washington Street, offered each tenant four stories of rooms. Bernard Donnelly, nephew and namesake of Kansas City's pioneer priest, built Donnelly Flats at Eighth and Oak streets.

Judge C. C. Quinlan, a successful cattleman, built the ornate Quinlan Apartments at Eighth Street and Highland Avenue. (An inveterate poker player who sometimes lost as much as $100,000 a game, Quinlan made one bet too many and lost the apartments.)

The Belmont Flats had a less impressive address — 15th Street and Tracy Avenue — and less ornate design, and the McClure Flats, a solid block from 19th to 20th streets, Grand Avenue to McGee Street, were built for workers in downtown businesses and railroads in the West Bottoms. These apartments started the trend to less ornate, more functional apartments built after the turn of the century.

The 1942 *Kansas City Social Register* described the Knickerbocker Apartments as "a country home in the heart of the Broadway district." Located just south of the Kansas City Life Insurance Company on Knickerbocker Place, the three-story brick and cut stone buildings were constructed in 1910. The architect was Leon Grand Middaugh, who also designed the Westport Library at 118 Westport Road.

Older, turn-of-the-century apartments, hugged the sidewalk without even a hint of a yard and were more ornate in design. The siting and design of the Knickerbocker Apartments was considerably different from the flats that were built before and just after the 1900s. These apartments were set back from the sidewalk, allowing a front yard, and were designed of simple, straight lines.

The concept was to provide more space for family living. Many contained eight rooms, including three bedrooms, a breakfast room and a living room with a fireplace. Another appealing feature was the lack of traffic on the streets. Knickerbocker Place was a private street until it was deeded to the city in 1958.

The most striking feature was the streetscape, the "mirror" effect obtained by the apartment buildings facing one another the length of the block. This effect was destroyed in 1982 when Kansas City Life Insurance Company, which owned the buildings, received city approval to demolish the north side and build its computer center on the site. The south side apartment buildings survive.

TULLIS PLACE, Eighth and Jefferson streets. Today the exclusive River Club occupies part of the site.
Kansas City, Missouri Public Library - Missouri Valley Special Collections

BELMONT FLATS, 15th Street and Tracy Avenue, looked like a fortress. Today the downtown loop of Interstate 70 cuts through the south part of the apartment's site.
Kansas City, Missouri Public Library - Missouri Valley Special Collections

A t the turn of the century, the Armour family was one of the richest in town. Simon B. Armour and his brother Phillip came to Kansas City in 1870, just as the livestock industry was developing in the West Bottoms. The Armours opened their packing plant there in 1871. Enlarged several times, Armour and Company became one of the largest meat packing houses in the country.

Simon Armour settled above the West Bottoms on Quality Hill, building a house on the west side of Broadway between 12th and 13th streets. Later he moved south, helped start the Hyde Park neighborhood and built a mansion on 35th Street (now Armour Boulevard).

Kirkland Armour, Simon's nephew, also settled on Quality Hill, building a home in 1884 for his bride, Annie Hearne of West Virginia, at 1017 Pennsylvania Avenue. To emphasize that this was a house for his bride, he had sculptured heads of Romeo and Juliet incorporated into the decorations on either side of the terra cotta archway of the home. (No explanation survives about why he ordered the sculptured face of a leering satyr for the archway above a large front window.)

Guests were received in the front parlor; it and the dining room had cherry woodwork and tiled fireplaces. Artwork on the tile portrayed Greek gods and characters from Shakespearean plays. The huge back parlor, where the family relaxed, had an applewood mantel and trim. A large mirror around the fireplace ran to the ceiling, stained glass windows and transoms decorated the house, and the staircases had balustrades of cherry.

Kirkland Armour had a country house, too. He built a manor house at 68th Street and Pennyslvania Avenue, surrounding it with servants quarters, barns and other farm buildings. He raised Hereford cattle on his 1,000 acres in what was rural Jackson County. The house is still there, but when the city grew south, the farmland was too valuable for grazing. Armour sold the land, which was developed into residential additions known as Armour Hills, Armour Fields, and Romanelli Gardens.

Like his uncle, Kirkland decided to leave Quality Hill. He moved south in 1893 and built a $125,000 mansion at 24 East Armour Boulevard. After Simon Armour's death, Kirkland succeeded him as president of the packing company. But he didn't have long to enjoy the job. He died at the age of 47, less than two years after his uncle's death.

The house at 1017 Pennsylvania Avenue became a boarding house and was razed in the late 1950s.

KIRKLAND ARMOUR Residence, 1017 Pennsylvania Avenue. Built 1884; demolished late 1950s. Now a surface parking lot.
Kansas City, Missouri Public Library - Missouri Valley Special Collections

Hudson and Oldsmobile automobiles were sold from the BRACE BUILDING 2623-29 Grand Avenue. Built 1917; demolished 1981.
Landmarks Commission of Kansas City, Missouri

PACKARD BUILDING, 2735 Main Street, Built 1930; demolished 1981. Now an empty lot.
Wilborn & Associates

This two-seater 1899 PACKARD was built three years after the introduction of the first successful American gasoline-powered automobile.
Kansas City, Missouri Public Library - Missouri Valley Special Collections

*A*uto dealerships flourished in Kansas City, particularly in an area between 15th and 28th streets from McGee to Main streets. Many related businesses, such as auto parts suppliers and battery shops were also located in that area.

The Brace Building at 2623-29 Grand Avenue was built in 1917. It was designed by architects McKecknie & Trask for the Security Realty Company to house the Hudson-Brace Motor Company. The facades, done in red brick tapestry design, contained terra cotta decorative detailing, and the first floor featured big display windows. When production of the Hudson ended, Brace acquired an Oldsmobile dealership and continued in business. The site is now a part of a project to straighten Grand Avenue.

The red brick Nash Motor Company Building, in the same area, was built in 1920 by the Collins Brothers from designs by

This 1919 NASH AUTOMOBILE was manufactured by the Nash Motor Company, founded in 1916 by Charles W. Nash (1864-1948).
Kansas City, Missouri Public Library - Missouri Valley Special Collections

the Nash engineering division. It was demolished in 1982.

The Packard Building at 2735 Main Street was completed in 1930. This masonry building was designed by Albert Kahn of Detroit for the Reid-Ward Motor Company, a Packard dealer. Five large glass windows for display dominated the front facade that faced Main Street. Inscribed in the cornice above the central entrance was the word "Packard." In 1947 the building was sold to a Packard dealer from Dallas, Texas. After the dealership was dissolved, the building had several tenants. The luxury automobile went out of production in 1958.

J. C. HIGDON, a well-known patent attorney, became in 1896 the first horseless carriage owner in Kansas City. The car was electric. Note the chain under the car that drove the wheels.
Kansas City, Missouri Public Library - Missouri Valley Special Collections

An early TRAFFIC REGULATION LAMP located at the intersection of Harrison and Armour boulevards. Though a simple mechanism, it was sufficient to control the few existing automobiles.
Kansas City, Missouri Parks and Recreation Department

T he automobile age in Kansas City got off to a shaky start when in May of 1901 the only two automobiles in the city crashed into each other. Dr. A. H. Cordier in the driver's seat of his Locomobile steamer and his passenger, Dr. Eugene Carbaugh, were heading toward downtown at a fast pace of 15 miles per hour. At the same time, Herbert A. Walpole, with his passenger, Ray Oliver, were in his steamer driving in the opposite direction. Each dared the other to give the right-of-way, each lost control and the automobiles collided near the intersection of 11th and Oak streets *The Kansas City Star* described the accident with the following:

> It was a bright and
>   cheerful day
> along sometime in early
>   May —
> no hint was there of any
>   great event
> As, sputtering and nearly
>   spent
> Two steamer cars,
>   emitting smoke
> Approached Eleventh
>   and Oak;
> They met with a careen-
>   ing lurch
> A short way from the
>   Christian Church.
> And so, in Nineteen
>   Hundred One,
> This Age of Crashes was
>   begun.

By 1906, Kansas City was among a number of Midwestern towns that were manufacturing automobiles. These include the Kansas City Motor Company, which made passenger cars and trucks. The passenger car had a four-cylinder engine and a double chair drive. Few roads had been paved, so most were rough and muddy. To combat the mud, the cars were made with high wheels and narrow tires, much in the fashion of a farmer's horse-drawn buggy. In 1910, the Kansas City Vehicle Company produced the Gleason, and the following year the Kansas City Motor Company made and sold the Stafford.

This early auto-making industry waned, but the car's influence continued and grew. As the number of cars on the road increased, traffic control became more important. The first traffic lights, in 1911, were simple warning lights. The first automatic traffic light was installed in June 1924 at 18th and McGee streets. Later that year, signals were added along McGee from the to 20th streets. (Nevertheless, Julien H. Harvey, director of the Kansas City Safety Council, advised motorists to avoid left-hand turns, a constant source of accidents, whenever possible.)

By 1912 there were more than 5,000 cars in Kansas City. Theft became a problem. In late 1915 a group of motorists formed the Anti-Motor Theft Association. The 500 members were readily identified by an emblem attached to their car's radiators. The group's president, Frank E. Lott, said the association was so successful after its first year that car thefts had gone down 60 percent — and theft insurance premiums were reduced by 20 percent. Members were merciless with the guilty, and paroles for those convicted were granted only upon the Association's recommendations.

BALTIMORE HOTEL, BALTIMORE BETWEEN 11TH AND 12TH

BALTIMORE HOTEL

I f ever Kansas City had a "Grand Hotel" it was the Baltimore. The hotel belonged to a time that measured luxury in terms of marble and space. Architect Louis S. Curtiss planned the building as a showplace of the Middle West, and it was the center of downtown social activities until the 1930s.

The six-story hotel was built in 1899 on property owned by the Thomas Corrigan estate. An additional two floors were added and an 11-story wing was built, extending the hotel south to 12th Street.

Architect Curtiss was said to have combined the originality of Frank Lloyd Wright with the traditional styles of Louis Sullivan. The hotel's Italian Renaissance style exterior may have been traditional, but the interior spoke of opulence. (Some said it was a nightmare of useless extravagances, an example of Curtiss' inclination for superfluous effects.) The 11th Street lobby, all marble and onyx, was done in Roman Empire decor. Green Messinian marble columns with gilt capitals supported the balcony, and ceilings were sculptured with designs. Red plush settees throughout reflected the color scheme: deep red, green and old ivory. The hotel crest, adapted from the coat of arms of Lord Baltimore, appeared everywhere.

Public rooms were immense, and a series of private dining rooms were especially suited for couples who wanted to be wined and dined (ladies were not admitted to the hotel bar, and would cause scandals if they were seen drinking in public.)

The Champagne Era crowd chose to entertain at the Baltimore for almost three decades. Peacock Alley, the name given to the hotel's block-long lobby, was the place to see the wealthy, dressed in evening gowns and tuxedos, parading to the city's most brilliant parties.

Another alley, Highball Alley, was the tunnel 10 feet wide and eight feet high between the hotel and the Willis Wood Theater, on the northwest corner of 11th Street and Baltimore Avenue. It saved steps for theatergoers, but women complained about having to pass through both the hotel bar and the men's smoking room in the theater to avoid inclement weather. (During the intermissions, men would head for the hotel bar for a drink. When they returned to their theater seats, the men were not always sober.)

The Baltimore's chef, Adrian Delvaux, had formerly been head chef at New York's Waldorf Hotel. Delvaux's talents won the praises of the Baltimore's guests, including famed tenor Enrico Caruso, who insisted on his visits to the hotel that Chef Delvaux personally prepare his favorite spaghetti.

The Baltimore merged with the Muehlebach Hotel in 1919. In 1928, Barney Allis, the Muehlebach's new owner (for whom the present-day Allis Plaza Hotel is named), took over management of the hotel. But the Baltimore's reign as the grand hotel was ended. Its closing in 1938 marked the end of an era.

The lobby of the BALTIMORE HOTEL.
Kansas City, Missouri Public Library - Missouri Valley Special Collections

BALTIMORE HOTEL, east side of Baltimore Avenue between 11th and 12th streets. Built 1899; demolished 1939. Now the site of City Center Square.
Native Sons Collection

OLD WELL, 1605 Northwest Barry Road.
Robert Noback, photographer

*STERLING PRICE Residence, 1501
Northwest Barry Road. Built about
1870. It was purchased around 1930
by John K. Samuel, a descendent of the
owner of the early Indian trading post.*
Robert Noback, photographer

*GENERAL STORE, 1800 Northwest
Barry Road. Built about 1827.*
Robert Noback, photographer

BARRY COMMUNITY

*N*amed for William Taylor Barry, postmaster general of the United States under President Andrew Jackson, Barry was a community north of the Missouri River that had its beginnings about 1820. Among the few early structures was a hand-hewn log Indian trading post erected on a line between Indian Territory and what in 1821 became the state of Missouri.

The Indians, primarily Sac and Fox, were losing more and more land to the white settlers. They traded mainly furs for goods and whiskey. Since the white man was not supposed to sell whiskey to the Indians, a bottle would be placed on the bar at the trading post; soon it would be gone and in its place would be furs.

Among the early buildings in the Barry Community was a general store at what is now 1800 Northwest Barry Road. It was built about 1827. Several accounts of the area cite it as having been "the oldest continuously operated store west of the Mississippi River." Other buildings housed a tailor, harness and saddle shops. There also were two churches, a dry goods store and several saloons. Judge Thomas Chevis maintained an inn and horse stable. (The inn was donated to Jackson County and reassembled at Missouri Town 1855.)

This settlement was the only stagecoach stop on the road between Liberty Landing and Fort Leavenworth military post. Known then as Military Road, a part of the Oregon Trail, the road was built by troops from the fort and was heavily traveled by officers and their wives going to enjoy the social amenities of Liberty, Missouri. Army children were frequently sent to Liberty's private schools. The trip took a day, meaning a stop at the Barry Community's well — hand dug in 1825 — was inevitable.

Of later importance was a building at 2000 Northwest Barry Road that housed the Rising Sun Masonic Lodge No. 18. The lodge, originally known as the Smith Lodge, was built in 1851. Andrew S. Truman, Harry S. Truman's grandfather, was initiated there in 1859. An early Gothic Revival style house at 1501 Northwest Barry Road once belonged to Sterling Price, a nephew of General Sterling Price, a Confederate officer and former governor of Missouri. It was built about 1870 and renovated in 1933.

Considerable development in the area, annexed by Kansas City in 1959, made Barry Road a heavily traveled east-west thoroughfare. Narrow and hilly, it had been the scene of many traffic accidents. When the city began widening the road in 1986, most traces of the Barry Community were removed.

MISS BARSTOW'S SCHOOL, 15 Westport Road. Built 1899; demolished 1929. Now the site is a surface parking lot.

The Barstow School

Miss Mary L. C. Barstow and Miss Ada C. Brann founded The School for Girls (now THE BARSTOW SCHOOL) at 1204 Broadway in 1884.
The Barstow School

*M*iss Ada Brann and Miss Mary L. C. Barstow must have felt both anxiety and excitement in 1884 as they journeyed west to Kansas City. They had been invited by several wealthy businessmen to open a school that would prepare their daughters for entrance into eastern colleges. Recent graduates of Wellesley College, they were well qualified for the positions.

The School for Girls opened that same year in a house at 1204 Broadway. Five pupils were enrolled the first day. Classes were held in a bare front parlor with only five chairs and a blackboard. Miss Brann taught mathematics, history and English, while Miss Barstow was responsible for Latin, Greek and Anglo-Saxon.

As enrollment grew, more space was needed, so the school moved frequently in the next few years. It remained on Quality Hill, though, and accepted boys who wanted to prepare, according to the school's advertisements, for Harvard, Yale and Princeton but had no private school of their own to attend.

Community support was strong. Kansas City was enjoying a time of prosperity. Eastern capital was rolling into the city and fortunes were being made. The school's future looked secure, but by the late 1890s the school's wealthy clientele was moving south. The school, now known as the Kansas City Day and Home School, moved temporarily to the Allen Library on Westport Road while awaiting completion of its new home at 15 Westport Road. It may have been at this temporary location when the school caught the fancy of William Rockhill Nelson, founder of *The Kansas City*

Star, whose daughter, Laura, attended the school. With his belief in education and high hopes for the future, Nelson became a generous contributor to the new building.

Architect Adriance Van Brunt designed the spacious Colonial Eclectic style yellow and white frame structure. It looked out over a large lawn with traces of an old apple orchard. Grades from kindergarten through high school enjoyed ample classroom space, an assembly hall and a gymnasium. By this time there were several private boys schools in the city, so the school again was exclusively for girls.

Just before the move, Miss Brann announced she was returning east. Miss Barstow, at the urging of Nelson, agreed to remain. With the move came a new name: Miss Barstow's School. It flourished on Westport Road. The school reflected Miss Barstow's academic goals: small classes, independent thought and a solid curriculum.

Two students who attended classes at the Westport building became famous. Bess Wallace, who became Mrs. Harry S. Truman, attended one year of post-graduate classes in 1905. Harlean Carpenter, later known to moviegoers as Jean Harlow, began kindergarten in 1915 and stayed through fifth grade.

When Miss Barstow retired in 1923, many wondered if the school would survive without her. The board of trustees believed it could, and began a $150,000 fund-raising drive to buy property for a new complex at 50th and Cherry streets. The Barstow School moved in 1924 into three buildings at that site (now part of Midwest Research Institute) and remained there until it moved in 1962 to its present location at 115th Street and State Line Road.

BELLECLAIRE APARTMENT HOTEL, 401 East Armour Boulevard Built 1927; demolished 1979.

Sherry Piland

BELLECLAIRE
APARTMENT HOTEL

*I*n the late 1890s and early 1900s, Armour Boulevard — originally only a dirt road — was a street of "swagger homes" (built to last a century) and "smart entertainment," of landaus, pony phaetons, tandems and traps. When the Hyde Park addition was platted in the late 1880s it was known as Commonwealth Avenue. Then, shortly after Kirkland Armour built his home in 1893, the street took his name. During his lifetime, the principal social life of the city radiated in all directions from Kirkland Armour's home.

Area property owners read like a "Who's Who" of Kansas City: Dr. J. D. Griffith, Thomas H. Mastin, Jacob L. Loose, E. H. Leo Thompson, Andrew Drumm, Joseph T. Bird, Henry Van Brunt and Fred Harvey.

Gradually, the character of the boulevard began to change as a result of the city's growth. The era of the automobile made access to outlying areas easier and permitted more southern residential districts to develop. This altered forever one of the most important streets in the newly laid-out boulevard system. The day came when most of the old Armour Boulevard residences fell at the hands of wrecking crews. The streetscape and skyline underwent a startling

change. In the place of wonderful houses rose "towering" hotels and apartment buildings. Among those was the Belleclaire Apartment Hotel, 401 East Armour Boulevard, completed in 1927 and designed by Nelle E. Peters, Kansas City's most prominent woman architect.

Peters was a remarkable architect, particularly for the time in which she practiced. The idea of a woman designing buildings was, by and large, unacceptable to the public. To help circumvent this prejudice, Peters (like other local woman architects) was noted in the city building permits by initials N. E. Peters. She remained undaunted by the male-dominated profession, as is proven by the hundreds of buildings — many yet standing — that sprang from her drawing board.

The Belleclaire, a 10-story building on the southeast corner of Armour Boulevard and Gillham Road, provided a style of living that is no longer sought. Apartments that many years ago were

the equivalent of home living were lost to the present-day suburban mentality.

The Belleclaire was vacant for several years, during which time it was struck by a number of questionable fires. At 8:45 a.m. Sunday, May 5, 1979, with the help of 240 dynamite charges, the building was taken down. A small landscaped park now occupies the site.

It took only seconds for dynamite to fell the BELLECLAIRE APARTMENT HOTEL, that had become an eyesore, ravaged by neglect and years of vacancies.
Jim Lewin

Senator Thomas Hart Benton, for whom BENTON SCHOOL was named. He served for 30 years in The United States Congress as a Democratic senator from Missouri.
Kansas City, Missouri Public Library - Missouri Valley Special Collections

*I*n 1880, ten years after it opened, Benton School had an enrollment of more than 1,000 students. By 1908, only 65 were enrolled. What happened?

The two-story, 12-room schoolhouse was in the West Bottoms, surrounded by homes of immigrants, many of whom worked in nearby factories, packing plants, warehouses and the stockyards. It was a small, self-sufficient community with churches, shops and professional services. Residents rarely needed to venture to the top of the bluffs for anything.

The 1880s started as good years. By the early 1880s, the West Bottoms seemed on its way to being an important residential and commercial area. But the loss of its residences was its undoing. Principal Emma C. Farren told of 52 houses being demolished to make way for a freight depot for the Missouri, Kansas & Texas Railroad Company. Soon after that, the Rock Island Railroad Company took out an entire block for its needs. Residents who were displaced moved away instead of buying other houses in the area. Since business was there to stay, land became too expensive for residential use. As more and more land went to industrial use, residents fled.

In 1903 the Benton School name was transferred to a new elementary school at 30th Street and Benton Boulevard. The school in the West Bottoms remained open as the West Kansas School until 1912. The site is now a vacant lot in a shadow cast by "progress": Interstate 670.

B'NAI Jebudah OAK STREET TEMPLE, on the southwest corner of 11th and Oak streets. Built 1884. Farewell services were held June 5, 1908. Commercial buildings occupy the site today.
Congregation B'Nai Jehudah

B'NAI JEHUDAH
OAK STREET TEMPLE

W ith the arrival about 1840 of the "Messrs. Cahn & Block," Kansas City Jewry had its beginning. They opened a trading post on the levee at what was known as Westport Landing. During the ensuing years, more Jews arrived, including Louis Hammerslough, who came in 1858 from Springfield, Illinois, to open a branch of his family's clothing manufacturing business. Hammerslough was for many years an active participant in the civic activities of the city.

The first Jewish organization of note was the formation in 1865 of the Hebrew Benevolent Society of Kansas City. Organized with the intent of carrying on traditional burial services, the society had accumulated enough money by May 1866, to buy land at 18th and Lydia streets for a cemetery.

Before worship services were regularly scheduled, Jews had met only twice a year, in the fall, for Rosh Hashanah and Yom Kippur. In 1870, with 25 families as charter members, Congregation B'nai Jehudah, meaning son of Judah, was formed. Benjamin A. Feinman served as the first president. Services were held, at first, in the Masonic Hall at Fourth and Walnut streets. In the late 1870s, the women of the congregation organized the city's first charity, the Hebrew Ladies' Relief Society. In 1875 the congregation moved into a frame synagogue on the southeast corner of Sixth and Wyandotte streets.

By 1875 the congregation had more than doubled. Under the leadership of Rabbi Joseph Krauskopf, it grew not only in membership but also financially, and a lot at the southwest corner of 11th and Oak streets was purchased for $5,500. The old temple was sold and work on the new one began in 1883. Constructed at a cost of $30,000, the Moorish style brick temple with twin cupolas opened Friday, September 4, 1884. On the next night the festivities concluded with a banquet at the Progress Club on Quality Hill, forerunner of the Oakwood Country Club. In 1890, side galleries were added, increasing the temple's capacity to more than 900 worshippers.

Over the years the temple's membership and influence grew, particularly under the leadership of Dr. Harry H. Mayer, a young rabbi who had come to Kansas City in 1899 from Little Rock, Arkansas. In 1905 a committee approved purchase of a new site on the southwest corner of Linwood Boulevard and Flora Avenue. The new temple, designed by the local architectural firm of Howe, Hoit & Cutler, was dedicated in September 1908, three months after final services were held at the old synagogue. Part of the stone foundation of the old temple at 11th and Oak streets can still be seen.

BOARD OF TRADE 210 West Eighth Street. Built 1888; demolished 1968.   Kansas City, Missouri Public Library - Missouri Valley Special Collections.

BOARD OF TRADE

There is some question as to when the Board of Trade was organized: February 6, 1856, or February 6, 1869. In 1856 a small group of businessmen banded together, calling themselves the Board of Trade. However, they were not involved in daily grain transactions, but acted as advocates of the city's commercial interests. The following year they became known as the Commercial Club, the forerunner of the Chamber of Commerce. A new Board of Trade came into existence in 1869, dealing with grain commodities. Officers were elected and regular meetings were held in the trading hall, a dingy room on Union Street, across from the West Bottom's Union Depot. The prime commodity was corn; wheat was secondary.

In 1870, Kansas City was a rapidly growing metropolis with the business district centered around Sixth and Delaware streets. Aware of that, and outgrowing the old office on Union Street, the Board of Trade moved in 1877 into a new building on the corner of Fifth and Delaware streets. The three-story building was designed by Asa Beebe Cross, who had designed St. Patrick's Catholic Church and Rectory at 800 Cherry Street several years earlier.

The next expansion came in 1887, to another new building on the northwest corner of Eighth and Wyandotte streets. That building, the winner of an architectural competition attracting more than 50 entries, was designed by the Chicago firm of Burnham & Root. Although the firm designed a number of buildings in Kansas City, only one is known to survive: the William C. Scarritt residence at 3240 Norledge Avenue, also built in 1888.

The seven-story, H-shaped Board of Trade Building cost $700,000 to build. Two wings were connected by a grand entrance arch and a skylighted concourse. The grain trading hall was behind the two-story arched windows in the west wing's fifth floor. For many years the Chamber of Commerce, originally the Commercial Club, was also located in the building.

The Board of Trade shared in Kansas City's rapid growth after World War I. By the early 1920s the many departments and grain firms had outgrown the building, frequently finding needed space in adjacent structures. In 1925, a move was made into a 14-story building at 10th and Wyandotte streets, built by Mrs. Rodella Dwight Lease under an agreement with the board and its members. The board remained there until 1964, when it moved south to 49th and Main streets, its present location.

For many years after the board moved, the building at Eighth and Wyandotte streets was known as the Manufacturers Exchange Building. It was demolished in 1968. An eight-story commercial building occupies the site.

BOARD OF TRADE'S trading room occupied the entire fifth floor of the west wing. On the sixth floor level was a small balcony where spectators could observe trading activities.
Kansas City, Missouri Public Library - Missouri Valley Special Collections.

VICTOR BUCK RESIDENCE on the northeast corner of 12th and Washington streets. Built 1879. The Cathedral Towers, a retirement home, is on this corner.
Kansas City, Missouri Public Library - Missouri Valley Special Collectons.

VICTOR BUCK RESIDENCE

*K*ansas City has had several houses designed by celebrated architects. Two Frank Lloyd Wright houses still are standing: one north of the Missouri River and one in the Valentine neighborhood. One house known to have been designed by Stanford White, the noted New York architect, was on the northeast corner of 12th and Washington streets.

White was an important influence on American architecture. But his place in history is marked by his murder. In 1906 he was shot, in full view of hundreds of people in Madison Square Garden, by Harry K. Thaw. White had been having an affair with Thaw's wife, actress Evelyn Nesbitt.

The home at 12th and Washington streets was built in 1879 for Victor B. Buck, who had made a fortune in the wholesale boot and shoe business in St. Joseph, Missouri, and whose immense wealth included gold and silver mines in Colorado. He moved his family to Kansas City and in 1879 commissioned one of the best-known architectural firms in the country to design his Quality Hill mansion. White had just become the third member of the famed New York partnership of McKim, Mead & White, which later designed Kansas City's New York Life Building at Ninth Street and Baltimore Avenue.

White designed the house in the Second Empire style. The architect's special interest was interior design. The three floors of the Buck home had soaring ceilings and high windows, characteristic of American architecture of the period. The rich mahogany paneling of interior walls and various sculptural features showed White's flair for decorative arts.

White designed two large crystal chandeliers to hang in a hall lined with floor-to-ceiling mirrors. At night the reflections from the two parlors facing the mirrors gave those attending Buck's parties the illusion that the house was larger than it was.

Victor Buck's daughter died in the early 1890s. Grief-stricken, Buck moved his family to Connecticut. The house was sold to Dr. C. Hiram Carson, regarded by many as a medical miracle worker of the day, who turned the mansion into The Temple of Health. Carson filled a room full of crutches, telling would-be patients that they were left by patients he had cured. After Carson's death, another doctor, this one with a better reputation, bought the home and turned it into a private sanitarium.

In the late 1940s the mansion became a restaurant with the unlikely name of "Down-the-Alley-and-Through-the-Kitchen."

CASTLE RIDGE

C astle Ridge, one of the city's greatest showplaces, attested to the financial success of its owner, Dr. Isaac M. Ridge, as well as to the ostentation of the 1880s.

Ridge, born in Kentucky, moved with his family in 1834 to Dover, Missouri. He attended school there, then went to Transylvania University in Lexington, Kentucky, where he was graduated with honors in 1848. He arrived in Kansas City that same year and opened an office on Main Street and the levee. He wasn't the first physician in the area — Dr. Benoist Troost had gone into practice here in 1844.

A year after he began practice, a deadly plague struck the area. It was believed to have initially been carried in on riverboats and later by wagon trains. Belgian immigrants in the East Bottoms were struck particularly hard. Ridge worked tirelessly among patients including Indians as well as settlers, stopping only when he, too, contracted the disease. In

appreciation of his care, the Indians gave him the name of "Little Thunder" and made him an honorary member of the Wyandotte tribe.

Ridge served as the city physician during the Civil War. He retired from medicine in 1873, having decided to invest in real estate. It was in land that he made his fortune.

In 1882, he built a mansion for his second wife on a 40-acre tract, set back from the southeast corner of 21st Street and Woodland Avenue, only a few blocks north of the city limits. The house was primarily of Ridge's own design. The three-story house cost $75,000 and had 30 rooms, including a third-floor ballroom. The ornamental brick exterior had cut-stone trim, and it was said that the spires of Independence could be seen from the tower on a clear day.

Ridge died at his castle in 1907. His wife, Margaret D. Ridge, lived there until her death in 1923. The house was later occupied by the Western Baptist College It was demolished in 1930 for the construction of Lincoln High School.

CENTRAL HIGH SCHOOL, 11th and Locust streets. Original structure was built in 1892. The fire escape was added in 1933. The Municipal Court of Appeals and the City Police Headquarters Building now occupy the site.   Jackson County Historical Society

CENTRAL HIGH SCHOOL /
KANSAS CITY JUNIOR COLLEGE

*C*ontroversy surrounding Kansas City's School Board's decisions are not new. When Central High School, the city's first public high school, opened in 1867, it was met with opposition. Realizing the need for a public high school, the Board of Education voted to open one in a building next to Humboldt School, an elementary school. When this became known, parents and taxpayers revolted. Dr. Isaac M. Ridge, leader of the "pullbacks" or objectors, said a high school was "unnecessary folderol and a waste of public money." The "Pamperers," those who favored a high school, were accused of "pampering young folks" and told that high school "would put foolish notions in their heads." The board gave in to public pressure. Although the school opened, its name was only Central School. The district experimented with night classes at Central during the 1870s, when E. C. White was principal. They were judged unsuccessful because "the conduct of the white boys was intolerable."

The first graduating class was in 1873, a class of five out of an enrollment of about 100. Graduation exercises were held in the Coates Opera House. As the enrollment grew, additions were made to the building, but there still was not enough space. A new building was constructed in 1883, but less than 10 years later it, too,

was overcrowded. It was razed and in 1892 the building that became a familiar sight to Kansas Citians was erected at 11th and Locust streets.

It was a handsome, four-story, Romanesque style brick building. The most imposing features were the tall spire and a copper-domed observatory, complete with a telescope. The telescope was very popular until the trolley lines were installed on 12th Street. The passing streetcars created severe vibrations that rendered the telescope all but useless.

Central High School had several famous alumni, including baseball great Casey Stengel and actor William Powell. Both were in the 1911 graduating class.

The school district used the new building until 1915, when the school moved to Linwood Boulevard and Indiana Avenue. That same year, Kansas City Junior College opened in the old high school. The building continued to look the same for many years. But in 1933, a curious addition was made to the exterior: a metal tube fire escape. It began on the fourth floor, where the assembly room was, and went to the ground.

Former students and teachers from Central High and the Junior College had one last chance to pass through the handsome wrought iron gates and climb the well-worn wooden stairs at the final reunion in 1949. Hundreds returned, eager for one last memory and a bit of nostalgia, before the building was demolished.

CENTROPOLIS HOTEL on the northwest corner of Fifth Street and Grand Avenue. Built 1880; demolished 1939.
Kansas City, Missouri Public Library - Missouri Valley Special Collections

CENTROPOLIS HOTEL

The Centropolis Hotel was named after a dream. William Gilpin, a friend of the builder, envisioned a great city, continuous from Independence to the Kaw River, and wanted the city to be named "Centropolis." This was in the 1840s — he was way before his time.

The builder of the Centropolis Hotel, Moses Broadwell, resembled his biblical namesake with his full, flowing beard. Before the Civil War, Broadwell owned 100 slaves who worked his large cotton plantation near Biloxi, Mississippi. He lost the plantation in the war's aftermath and came to Kansas City in the early 1870s. Broadwell married the daughter of Dr. Joseph Wood, the former Clay County, Missouri, physician who was Jesse James' surgeon.

Broadwell built a four-story brick Italianate style hotel on the northwest corner of Fifth Street and Grand Avenue in 1880. It was so successful that he soon added a five-story wing facing Fifth Street and later a six-story addition built on Grand Avenue that gave the hotel 141 sleeping rooms. The two Fifth Street wings were connected by an entryway that led into a courtyard, which gave the hotel distinction. To finance construction, Broadwell took on a silent partner, Dr. S. S. Laws, once president of the University of Missouri.

Broadwell's personal friend, Jefferson Davis, president of the Confederacy, stayed at the hotel on occasional visits to Kansas City — as did another guest, Ulysses S. Grant who had defeated the Confederacy. Presidents Chester A. Arthur and Grover Cleveland also were guests. Entertainers who were in town to perform at the nearby Gillis Theater stayed at the Hotel. Actor James O'Neill, father of playwright Eugene O'Neill, stayed there when in town, and prize fighter-turned performer, John L. Sullivan, was a frequent guest.

The Centropolis was the first hotel in Kansas City to add electricity when it became available. The long bar and dining room on the west side of the hotel were big attractions. The Kansas City Produce Exchange held its daily sessions and banquets there. Couples came for after-theater suppers and danced until dawn in the ballroom, where an orchestra played every night.

As new hotels were built farther south in the downtown area, the Centropolis began to fade. By World War I the hotel rented rooms by the week to transients. The west side of the hotel suffered structural damage during remodeling in 1923 and was torn down. In 1939 what remained was demolished and the land became part of a two-block extension of the east side of the City Market. These buildings are to be remodeled in the Riverfront redevelopment effort of 1990 to house a museum displaying recovered artifacts from a sunken 19th century riverboat.

CHACE SCHOOL, demolished in 1913, was located on the southwest corner of 14th Street and The Paseo. An Interstate 70 ramp casts its shadow on the site today. Kansas City, Missouri Public Library - Missouri Valley Special Collections.

THE CHACE SCHOOL

*C*onstructed in 1881, the red brick Romanesque style elementary school at 14th Street and Flora Avenue (now The Paseo) is distinguished not so much for its useful educational life as for the terms of its destruction. Chace School — named for Mayor Charles A. Chace, elected in 1880 on the Democratic ticket and a 10-year member of the School Board — was in the wrong place at the wrong time. The Paseo had become a fashionable street of mansions, and by 1911 the abandoned school was an eyesore. Area residents were eager to be rid of it. Voters defeated a bond issue that would have been used to move the building, and that sealed its fate.

The Board of Education approved the building's demolition under a very unusual agreement with the city's parks and water boards. Instead of selling the land for cash, the school board agreed to give the land to the city, specifically to the Park Department. In return, it got $25,000 of free water for its schools from the city — more than three times what the district used. It was replaced by a new Chace School constructed on the north side of 13th Street between Euclid and Garfield avenues.

ANNIE CHAMBERS House on the southwest corner of Third and Wyandotte streets. Built 1871; demolished 1942. Now the land is used for the parking lot of the Old Chelsea Adult Movie Theater.

Kansas City, Missouri Public Library - Missouri Valley Special Collections

*I*t might be a dubious honor, but from the 1870s until the 1920s, Kansas City was known to have one of the most elegant bordellos in the West and Midwest. This was the famous Annie Chambers' brothel at Third and Wyandotte streets. The lady herself has become a figure of folklore in the city's history. Annie's "house" has remained a fascinating topic of conversation for more than a century.

Kansas City had red-light districts from the 1850s. Men were coming through on their way to California's 1849 Gold Rush, hundreds of steamboat passengers landed at the levee at Grand Avenue, Santa Fe traders did business at the levee and the city was the end of the line for early railroads. The traffic of men in and out of the city numbered hundreds, maybe thousands, daily. Early saloons, brothels and gambling halls were money-making businesses.

Even before the Civil War, the public square at Fourth and Main streets was surrounded by these establishments. When the livestock trade and the Union Depot brought men to the West Bottoms, similar businesses opened there and flourished. In the riverfront town Wyandotte Street seemed to attract the better houses. Just west of Annie's was Eva Prince's house, and on the northwest corner of Third and Wyandotte streets was the mansion that Madam Lovejoy had spent $100,000 to build and furnish. But Annie's was the first on the block.

Leannah Loveall Chambers Kearns — alias, Annie Chambers.
Kansas City, Missouri Public Library - Missouri Valley Special Collections

Annie's real name was Leannah Loveall Chambers Kearns. She was born in Kentucky in 1842. After a series of tragedies, the death of her two children and her first husband — she turned to a childhood friend for help. The friend was a prostitute in an Indianapolis, Indiana, brothel. She invited Annie to join her. Within two years Annie owned a house of her own and, after being raided by the police decided to move to Kansas City.

Annie Chambers came to Kansas City in 1869, just after the Hannibal Bridge opened. She rented a house on the levee not far away from the bridge, invited a few girls to join her and opened for business. She prospered. After two years she bought a lot at Third and Wyandotte streets and built her own house.

The reason we know a good deal about Annie Chambers and her house is that shortly before she died in 1935 at the age of 92, she gave lectures and press interviews

about her life. Sitting in the faded glory of her parlor, she charged 50 cents a person to hear her story. She gave the money to the City Union Mission and later deeded her house to that organization.

Annie told her audiences about her house, a two-story, 24 room brick mansion with furnishings that came from the 1876 Philadelphia Centennial Exposition. The distinctive entrance was formed by concrete pillars resembling bamboo supporting a tiled roof. Annie said she got the idea from Chinese drawings.

Inside, the sycamore floors were kept highly polished. There were many Oriental rugs and in some rooms thick red carpet covered the floor. The windows were covered with vermilion velvet draperies. Annie's name was set in blue tile in the floor of the hallway, and over the stairway leading to the bedrooms upstairs was a filigreed piece of bronze with the initials "A. C." outlined in red lights. A front parlor was furnished with walnut chairs and sofas piled with richly textured cushions. There was a dining room (Annie's cook was the envy of several hotels) and the grand ballroom on the first floor had a canopied ceiling. Along three walls of the ballroom were "artistic" paintings of nude women and on the fourth wall were mirrors 10 feet high and 16 feet long.

In her lecture Annie said that

the number of girls who had worked for her over the years numbered in the thousands. Some of them had made as much as $200 a week plus gifts and commissions for all the liquor that was sold. She proudly said that many of them had gone on to happy marriages and that she got hundreds of letters from many who had married men they first met in her house.

By 1913, citizens were in an uproar about prostitution in Kansas City. A society for the prevention of commercialized vice was organized and pressure was put upon city officials to close down the brothels — an estimated 47 bordellos in the city employing as many as 248 girls. Under pressure, the police raided these houses and closed them down.

Annie Chambers asked to speak before a committee meeting of the society.

"Your movement is beginning at the wrong end," she said. "Throw the mantle of protection about the young girl before she has met her first fall. You wait until too late if you expect to accomplish much by reforming girls who have had the public stamp placed upon them by society. They come to us when they have no place else to go. Their parents have turned against them, the church gives them no welcome, their friends spurn them and society kicks them further down. We do not send for them. Ours is the haven of last resort."

The picture of Annie gives the impression that she was all business, but it would appear that the lady had a heart.

*CHANDLER BUILDING, 101 West 47th
Street, as it appeared in the 1930s.
Built 1916; demolished 1961. On the
right can be seen the Plaza Theater.
Today Swansons on the Plaza occupies
the floral company site.*
Wilborn & Associates

CHANDLER BUILDING

S ix years before the J. C. Nichols Company undertook Edward Buehler Delk's 1922 plan for the Country Club Plaza, the Chandler Building at 47th Street and Mill Creek Parkway (now J. C. Nichols Parkway) was built by Clarence A. Chandler, founder of the Chandler Landscape and Floral Company.

The company was first known as the Elmhurst Landscape and Nursery Company. In 1909 Chandler resigned as superintendent of Swope Park to join his brother Marshall in the company. Originally their store was at 35th and Main streets; the move to a new building made the company the first business on what was to become the Plaza.

The original 47th Street building was redesigned in 1920 to create its familiar curved front. The redesign was by Edward W. Tanner, who for many years was the principal architect for the Nichols Company.

The retail flower shop was on the first floor of the Spanish-style building. Leading off to the south was the door to the greenhouse. A nine-room suite on the second floor was occupied by five physicians. In 1927, the clubhouse of the Junior League of Kansas City, Missouri, occupied a part of the second floor before moving to its own building at 5815 Brookside Boulevard. (The club paid Fred Wolferman $1 a year for the building, along the streetcar tracks just north of his 59th Street store.) The club later moved to its present location at 4651 Roanoke Parkway.

In 1928, Nichols bought the Chandler property. The landscape and floral company remained a tenant until 1961, when the building and its distinctive smokestack were razed.

CYPRIEN CHOUTEAU'S HOUSE 412 Charlotte Street. Built about 1845;
demolished 1946. The bluffs are no longer there. Today the Heart of America
Produce Company warehouse is at that location.
Kansas City, Missouri Public Library - Missouri Valley Special Collections

CYPRIEN CHOUTEAU RESIDENCE

*C*yprien Chouteau was the younger brother of Francois Chouteau, the founder of Kansas City. Francois and Berenice Chouteau came by boat from St. Louis in 1821 to establish their fur trading settlement on the banks of the Missouri River.

Cyprien arrived a few years later, establishing a trading post on the Kaw River, about where Bonner Springs, Kansas, is today. He built four log buildings around an open square for protection and gave the settlement the name "Four Houses." In 1851 he married Nancy Francis, the daughter of a Shawnee chief. Cyprien and Nancy, who had been educated at a Quaker mission near Westport, had three children, Frederick, Edmond and Mamie.

In 1855 the family moved to a farm west of the Big Blue River at what today is 24th Street and Kensington Avenue. In 1865 they moved to the Town of Kansas to a two-story brick house of 10 rooms built by John Calvin McCoy at 412 Charlotte Street, on one of the bluffs above the Missouri River. It was customary to light lamps and put them in the upper windows to guide the steamboat captains on their way to the levee.

Cyprien's daughter, Mamie Chouteau Guinotte, lived there until 1942 and remembered that Indians frequently came to the house to see her father, either for a free meal or to borrow money. She said that sometimes, when her mother and father saw them coming, they would close the doors and hide, hoping to avoid having to make a loan. The Indians regarded this as sort of a hide-and-seek game, Chouteau's daughter recalled; they came into the house, looking in clothes closets, under beds and behind doors until they found her father and, laughing, pulled him out, shouting: "We found you!"

Cyprien Chouteau died at the house in 1879. Nancy lived until 1912. The house had been purchased by the Lillis family in the 1890s. When Charlotte Street was cut through the bluff, the house was left high on the edge of a cliff with a 35-foot drop on three sides to the street below. The precariously perched house survived, until 1946, as a connection to the Chouteau family which started the town more than a century before.

*When CITY HALL opened at 411 Main
Street in 1892, Mayor William S.
Cowherd's salary was $3,600 while
Thomas M. Speers, chief of police and
George C. Hale, fire chief, each
received $3,000 annually.*
Kansas City, Missouri Public Library -
Missouri Valley Special Collections

I f the many buildings that have served as Kansas City's town hall were lined up, side by side, they would provide a visual display of the city's growth from a raw town to a great Midwestern metropolis.

On February 22, 1853, the state legislature granted a charter to the the Town of Kansas (even though it was commonly called Kansas City the name was not changed officially until 1889.) For the next five years, its municipal government held most of its meetings on the second floors of a number of buildings along the levee.

Mayor M. J. Payne realized that a permanent building was essential for carrying out the city government's functions. Capitalizing on solid tax collections, the City Council passed an ordinance on October 13, 1856, authorizing the construction of a new city hall and a market house on the public square. J. W. Ammons (who a year later was elected to the council) was awarded the contract to build the two-story brick building at Fourth and Main streets. The first floor was to be divided between the city hall and the market house, and the second floor was for public meetings, dances and other social affairs. On Sundays it often was used for church services, since few of the denominations in the city had their own facilities.

City Hall went through several additions and alterations. Then, in early 1890, the council voted part of a $500,000 bond issue be spent on a larger city hall on the same site at 411 Main Street. William M. Taylor was awarded the contract to construct the six-story Romanesque style building. After the

old city hall was demolished, the city's business was conducted at the Exchange Building, 8th and Wyandotte streets.

The public square site, which had been a deep hollow filled over the years with trash and the dirt from leveling the bluffs behind the levee, was judged too unstable to bear the weight of such a large building. Louis S. Curtiss, an assistant superintendent of buildings under Simeon E. Chamberlain adopted a technique used in the construction of bridges. Sixty circular steel caissons resting on bedrock were filled with vitrified brick and cement. The vitrified brick was made at the Soldiers' Home in Leavenworth, Kansas, and was the first ever used in a Kansas City construction

project. Curtiss has, in several accounts of the building's construction, been credited with its design.

The city took occupancy October 24, 1892. By 1920, the city government needed even more space, and an annex was built, tucked between City Hall and Fire Station No. 25, which had been erected in 1908. When the citizens voted approval in 1931 of $32 million for public improvements, this spelled the final chapter for the old building. In 1937 the city offices were moved to the present city hall at 414 East 12th Street. The building, designed by Wight & Wight, has been cited nationally as a fine example of Art Deco style architecture.

The 1892 CITY HALL's council chambers.
Kansas City, Missouri Public Library - Missouri Valley Special Collections

*CITY MARKET, Fifth and Main streets
has been used as a public square from
the 1840s. The first farmer's stalls were
built in 1857. In this 1878 photo
farmers' wagons converge on the
square to unload their produce. The
business and governmental affairs of
the city revolved around the market
area until the 1940s but the square is
still the center for buying and selling
produce.*
Native Sons Collection

CITY MARKET

*T*he City Market has been in the same location since 1857. It was part of the land that Gabriel Prudhomme purchased from the federal government in the early 1820s. After he was murdered, Prudhomme's land was sold at auction to the Town Company and named the Town of Kansas.

Early settlers got water from the springs in a ravine 30 to 40 feet deep at the northeast corner of today's City Market. In 1855, the City Council voted to spend $10 for an iron water pump for the spring water. When roads were cut through the 80-to-100-foot bluffs directly behind the levee, the dirt removed was used to fill the ravine and cover the springs.

The Prudhomme land was platted into homesteads in 1838 and again in 1846 and sold off, piece by piece. The area that was to become Market Square was bought by the William Gillis family and in 1846 was given to the city for use forever by the public.

In 1857 the City Council granted a lease to Jacob and Fred Scheibel for $50 a year to operate a market on the square. The Scheibels built a series of wooden stalls on the east side, near Walnut Street. The Council allotted $4,637 to build a new City Hall and courthouse on the site. For the next 40 years, the town growth radiated from the public square.

The few sidewalks around the square were wooden. When it rained there was a sea of mud. Pigs allowed to run free came to the market looking for food and wallowed in the mud. In the summer of 1858 the market was so overrun with pigs that the council passed a "Hog Law." Thirty to 40 pigs roaming the streets were captured and put in the "hog pound."

The town was beginning to be civilized. Buildings surrounding the square accommodated businesses including stores, restaurants, hotels and theaters. Just a few blocks away on Pearl Street, the crest of the bluffs from Grand Avenue to Walnut Street, was the place the wealthy built their homes. After the gullies in the bluffs were widened into roads and mudslides caused the houses to lose ground, the rich moved to Quality Hill.

Main Street next to the square became known as "Battle Row" because of the violence bred by all the saloons and gambling houses there. On the second floor of the buildings were elaborately furnished private bars, faro banks, poker rooms and brothels. Heroes of western folklore — Wild Bill Hickock, Wyatt Earp, Bat Masterson, Buffalo Bill Cody and Doc Holliday spent time in the area. Jesse James frequented the Doggett House, a hotel on West Sixth Street near Walnut Street, and walked around the market without fear of being arrested, although he was recognized.

In 1888, the old stalls were taken down and a market building was built along Walnut Street from Fourth to Fifth streets. Later when a new City Hall was built on the west side of the square, the two buildings were connected by a walkway. The farmers backed their wagons to the edge of the buildings and sold their produce, much as farmers do today.

In 1940 the present market buildings were built on the same site. These buildings were remodeled in 1990. People still go to Fifth and Main streets to buy produce, and the use of Market Square is a living example of the continuity of Kansas City's history.

*COATES HOME in faded glory shortly
before it was torn down. A small
church is now located on the property
at 10th Street and Pennsylvaina
Avenue.*
Wilborn & Associates

KERSEY COATES RESIDENCE

*T*oday we know the area west of downtown as Quality Hill. But first it was called Coates Hill and Silk Stocking Ridge because wealthy people settled there. The first name was in honor of Kersey Coates who, on his first visit to Kansas City in 1854, bought 120 acres of land on the West Bluffs from Berenice Chouteau, wife of the city's first settler. Coates built his house on part of the land and developed the rest.

Colonel Coates (the military title was from the Civil War), was a champion of causes. A commanding figure, tall and lean, he was a leader in getting the Hannibal Bridge built over the Missouri River and bringing railroads into the city. He was a partner in banks, dry goods stores and brickyards. He built the magnificent Coates Opera House and the city's first modern hotel, the Coates House.

Coates came to the city as a representative of a group of Philadelphia capitalists interested in land investments. A staunch abolitionist, he also worked for the New England Emigrant Aid Society to help settle "free-staters" in the Kansas Territory.

After he bought the West Bluff land, Coates returned to Philadelphia, Pennsylvania, and married Sarah Walter Chandler. Sarah arrived April 15, 1856, on the steamboat William Campbell. Their daughter, Laura Coates Reed, published "In Memoriam, Sarah Walter Chandler Coates," a book of her mother's diaries and letters, in 1898. In it she quotes Sarah upon stepping onto the levee and seeing the ramshackle town: "And this is to be my home!"

The couple lived for a time in the Troost House Hotel. It was not unusual to hear bands of southern sympathizers outside shouting, "Death to all damned Yankees." Fearing for their lives, Coates kept a pistol under his pillow.

In 1859 the Coates moved into their two-story brick home on the southwest corner of 10th Street and Pennsylvania Avenue. It was Colonel Kersey Coates' street. He named it after his home state, paved it and built his house on it.

The house on high ground gave a good view of both the Kaw and Missouri Rivers. At the first sound of a boat's whistle, the household rushed to the verandas surrounding the house to identify the boat before it landed.

The Coates home became the center of the town's social life. It also would harbor anti-slavery advocates, and guns were stockpiled in the basement to defend against a Confederate attack.

During the Civil War, Coates, as a commander of the 77th Regiment in the Missouri militia, often was away. A battalion of Union soldiers, sent from Fort Leavenworth to establish Fort Union at 10th street and Broadway was visible from the east veranda of the Coates home. The soldiers used the foundation Coates had put in for his hotel to stable their horses. Even though a carelessly aimed cannonball fired from the fort dented the wall of the Coates home, Sarah was reassured by the soldiers' presence.

After the war, Coates built his hotel on the southeast corner of 10th street and Broadway, then built the Coates Opera House diagonally across the street. He lobbied the United States Congress for the Hannibal Bridge, went to Boston to convince the Hannibal, St. Joseph Railroad to come into the city once the bridge was finished and organized a group to buy land for the bridge and donate it to the city.

Coates also organized Kansas City's first fair in 1871, the precursor to the American Royal. People came from as far as 200 miles to see farm products, animals and equipment.

When Coates died in 1887, he was adding a south wing to his hotel. Sarah, who survived him by 10 years, saw that the addition was finished; another was added on the hotel's north side in 1889. (In January 1978, a fire destroyed the south wing killing 20 hotel residents. The remaining portion of the hotel has been restored and is used for offices and apartments.)

During the last 10 years of her life, Sarah Coates worked for the women's suffrage movement. Her friend Susan B. Anthony, the leader of the movement, was a frequent guest at the home.

After Sarah's death, the house was sold and by the turn of the century it had become a boarding house. In 1946 the home was remodeled to house the William Jewell Baptist Mission.

COLONEL KERSEY COATES - builder and civic leader.
Kansas City, Missouri Public Library - Missouri Valley Special Collections

COATES OPERA HOUSE northwest corner of 10th Street and Broadway. Built 1868/1870 and remodeled in 1881; destroyed by fire in 1901. Commercial buildings are now on the site.   Kansas City, Missouri Public Library - Missouri Valley Special Collections.

COATES OPERA HOUSE

*T*he opening of the Coates Opera House was a great step forward for the social life of Kansas City. Only after it opened did women dare to come regularly to the theater. Attending the Coates Opera House became the fashionable thing to do.

The Opera House and Coates House Hotel, across the street, were called the sentinels of Quality Hill. The theater opened October 8, 1870, with the production "Money." It was appropriately named. Colonel Kersey Coates spent $105,000 in constructing the theater modeled after the Detroit Opera House. It took two years, 300,000 feet of lumber and over one million bricks (made in the Coates brickyard at 12th Street and Broadway), to build the 97 by 110 foot building.

The theater was on the second floor. The first floor was occupied by a grocery and feed store. For the first time the city had a real stage, 36 by 72 feet (the largest in the West) and 10 dressing rooms for performers. The interior woodwork was of oak with a yellow pine floor. The audience sat on leather upholstered benches. The building had a stone foundation four feet thick, a grand mansard roof with heavy iron cornices, and niches in the front of the building that held statuary representing dramatic personages.

An earth dam was created by 10th Street to the south of the theater to hold back a deep pond. A wooden sidewalk that led to the theater became a muddy path when it rained. There were no paved streets, cable cars, or street lights in those days. Theatergoers walked up to the bluffs or came by carriages carrying coal oil lanterns to light their way home. On stormy nights the theater lobby had rows of muddy overshoes and lanterns.

Going to the Coates Opera House was more than entertainment, it was a social occasion. People went there to renew acquaintances and make new friends. Before the play and between acts there was much chatter and visiting. People waited in line for hours to get tickets. It was so popular that the theater was duplicated in St. Joseph, Missouri.

In 1881 Coates spent $45,000 to remodel the theater. He brought the stage down to the first floor and by creating a balcony and gallery, enlarged the capacity to 2,000. The benches were discarded and opera seats were put in. The theater was thought to be fireproof.. But on January 31, 1901, just one half hour after closing, a fire was discovered. Within an hour and a half, only a shell remained.

By this time four other first-class theaters had been built: The Gillis at Fifth and Walnut streets, The Grand at Seventh and Walnut streets, (both of these buildings still stand), The Auditorium at Ninth and Holmes streets and the Ninth Street Theater at Ninth and May streets. These and other theaters that came later owed a lasting tribute to Colonel Coates for making theater-going respectable.

To aid in raising funds to construct the "first" CONVENTION HALL, a gift concert was held. Donations included a piano, a gray donkey, a pair of Yorkshire pigs, and from Kirkland B. Armour a Hereford heifer, "Armour Rose."

Kansas City, Missouri Public Library - Missouri Valley Special Collections

P erhaps near the top of the list of Kansas City's triumphs is the construction of the two Convention Halls, with much of the credit due William Rockhill Nelson.

Nelson had decided the city needed a large auditorium suitable for conventions, concerts and other entertainment. Beginning in 1893, *The Kansas City Star* began taking this building campaign to the public. Slowly, public sentiment was won. In response to this, a meeting was called by the Commercial Club, forerunner of the Chamber of Commerce, on June 12, 1897. Enthusiasm grew so rapidly that a committee was immediately appointed to solicit funds. They decided at this meeting that the hall should not be constructed on leased ground. Instead, they would buy the site. And finally, the committee approved the issuance of stock in the project to all subscribers.

On December 2, 1897, a decision was made to build the hall at 13th and Central streets and an announcement was made that a prize competition for the best design would be held for the hall and that the cost of the building could not exceed $100,000. The prize was awarded to Frederick E. Hill, a local architect.

The first contract was let May 6, 1898. Construction progressed rapidly. The cornerstone was laid on August 11th, over a lead box that contained copies of local newspapers of that date and photographs of several prominent citizens. The box was retrieved January 30, 1937, by workmen supervising the razing of the building.

Reflected in the Classical style building was the spirit of Kansas City. When the hall opened on February 22, 1899, at a cost of $225,000, more than double the original estimate, it was debt-free. Citizens had subscribed every dollar.

It was a gala occasion, enjoyed by thousands. That afternoon John Philip Sousa, "the March King," conducted a band concert. In the evening there was another Sousa concert and a grand ball.

Expectations knew no bounds, for in early 1900 the Democratic National Committee selected Kansas City as the site for its national convention to begin July 4, 1900.

But about 1 p.m. April 4, 1900, a grocer, whose store was just a block away, saw smoke pouring out of the building. In an incredibly short time the hall was nothing but a mass of debris and tangled steel. Lathrop School, the Second Presbyterian Church and the Williamson flats, buildings adjacent to the hall, were heavily damaged.

Alerted almost immediately to the fire, the Democratic National Committee wired asking if Kansas City was still expecting to host the convention. The reply: "We will hold the Democratic Convention in Kansas City and we will have a Convention Hall by July 4."

These were ambitious words and a gamble, for there were many who believed such a feat would be impossible. Money, and the promise of more, rolled in. The problem then became how to get replacement material very quickly. Steel companies were cajoled and offered bonuses for prompt

The first CONVENTION HALL destroyed by fire April 4, 1900.
Kansas City, Missouri Public Library - Missouri Valley Special Collections

delivery. Appeals were made to railroads to allow each carload of steel the right-of-way over other traffic.

It was a frenetic time, with masons, carpenters and steel workers on day and night shifts. Unbelievably, "a 90 day miracle" happened, and Convention Hall opened as scheduled on July 4, 1900. On the fourth day of the convention, William Jennings Bryan received the nomination for president. Adlai Stevenson was nominated as his running mate. Bryan lost to the Republican nominee, William McKinley.

For the "new" CONVENTION HALL, also located on the northeast corner of 13th and Central streets "the wildest day in its history" was Armistice Day, November 11, 1918, when thousands of Kansas Citians gathered there to celebrate. The Auditorium Garage, topped by Barney Allis Plaza, now occupies the site.
Landmarks Commission of Kansas City, Missouri - Detroit Publishing Company

SECOND CONVENTION HALL

The day before the Democratic National Convention opened, the streets and sidewalks in front of Convention Hall were covered with debris and building materials. With so little time, emphasis was put on having the interior sufficiently finished to provide for the delegates' comfort. Crews worked around the clock and all of the litter was cleared by morning. The final exterior work was to be completed later.

The convention was a huge success. Kansas City looked upon the hall with justified pride.

Much credit for its success was due to manager Louis W. Shouse, who accepted the job on a temporary basis but stayed for over 30 years. To keep people coming to the hall, Shouse made extraordinary bookings that featured many famous entertainers of the day. Appearing in 1905 were opera stars Madame Nellie Melba and Enrico Caruso. All previous attendance records were broken when Sarah Bernhardt appeared in "Camille" in 1906. In 1921 the American Legion held a convention in the hall, with participants including United States General John J. Pershing and several European military leaders.

With the need for additional space and more modern facilities the city decided to build a new auditorium. An illustrated lecture by Admiral Richard E. Byrd, on his second Antarctic Expedition, was the last event in the hall. With the approval of the stockholders who had subscribed to the construction of the first hall, the Convention Hall Building Association sold the hall in 1935 to the city for $725,000. Seven hundred thousand dollars was returned to the city toward the completion of the Municipal Auditorium.

Demolition began on July 6, 1936. Crews removed the "century box" placing it behind a wrought-iron panel in the lobby of the Municipal Auditorium's Music Hall. It is to be opened by the mayor in the year 2000, presumably on the Fourth of July.

The French actress Sarah Bernhardt (1844-1923) appeared at CONVENTION HALL on February 28, 1906, in "Camille", her best known role. It was said that on that evening she appeared to her largest audience outside of France.
Kansas City Museum - Kansas City, Missouri

CRYSTAL PALACE, Agnes Avenue between 13th and 14th streets, looked like something out of a classic fairy tale but was not very practical. Hail and fire destroyed the building. Where once the palace stood is now undeveloped land.
Kansas City, Missouri Public Library - Missouri Valley Special Collections

CRYSTAL PALACE

*T*he Crystal Palace opened in 1887 with great fanfare, offering spectators a sight to behold. It went out in 1901 in the same way.

It was Kansas City's attempt at providing a permanent exposition building. It had a domed roof with 80,000 square feet of transparent glass: beautiful to look at but not very practical in a region that is subject to its share of hailstorms. Located on Agnes Avenue between 13th and 14th streets and surrounded by groves of walnut and papaw trees, it was built just beyond the city's limits. It was regarded as a reflection of Kansas City's spirit. However, its short life stood as an example of lack of planning and foresight.

James Goodin dreamed of duplicating the Crystal Palace of London. His idea caught the enthusiasm of the city's leaders, who held public meetings where committees were formed to raise the $260,000 needed. The palace was built in 100 days with bricklayers, carpenters and glazers working day and night, the darkness illuminated by gas and electric lights.

The building had 17 acres of floor space. It opened on October 7, 1887, with a grand flourish: President Grover Cleveland and his wife were on hand to make it official. At the opening fair, nearly all of the western, midwestern and southern states were represented by exhibits, and for the first time at such a fair there were also exhibits from Guatemala, Venezuela and Columbia. Machinery of every kind was on display, and thousands came to look at the building and the exhibits.

The exposition was followed by the Priests of Pallas parade around the Public Square. The Flambeau Club, the up-and-coming young men of town, had planned the parade to bring the visitors to the businesses around the square. Parades with bands, fireworks and floats lasted a week, and each evening there was a ball. The celebration, named after the Greek Goddess of Wisdom, Science and the Arts was an enormous success and continued for almost 40 years.

But the Crystal Palace did not last. By 1893 the building was empty and decaying, and hailstorms had broken every square foot of the glass roof. There were plans to blow up what remained with dynamite. But in August 1901, the building caught fire. That day in fields close by, hundreds had gathered to enjoy the Ringling Brothers Circus, and at 15th Street and Prospect Avenue, another crowd was sitting in the grandstand of a ballpark, watching a baseball game. The circus and ballgame were forgotten. Instead the crowds watched the spectacular fire. The flames could be seen far away, and thousands of people rushed from their neighborhoods to watch. Firemen decided to let the once magnificent building burn down. Flames melted away what was left of the glass, and the roof's supporting structure finally crashed down, leaving just a shell. The ruins were removed a short time later.

CYCLORAMA, Eighth and May streets, Built about 1884.
Kansas City, Missouri Public Library - Missouri Valley Special Collections

CYCLORAMA

Y ou might say the Cyclorama, built about 1884, was an early form of motion pictures: it gave Kansas Citians the opportunity to "experience" the Civil War battles of Missionary Ridge and Lookout Mountain. Scenes of battle actions were painted on floor-to-ceiling canvases that were hung along the inside walls of the building and made to move on a continuous roll. Viewers stood on a central platform in the hall and witnessed the battle progressing.

Abraham Judah, who had operated the Dime Museum at Ninth and Walnut streets, decided there was money in showing scenes of the Civil War battles. There were many Civil War veterans in town, and a younger generation that had interest in the battles. He purchased the canvases, which had been painted in Berlin.

Judah built the Cyclorama building at Eighth and May streets just east of Broadway and added mounds of dirt on the floor to resemble the battlefield terrain. It was said that the effect was so realistic, some women fainted while viewing the scenes. (Of course, swooning, or fainting, was quite in vogue in those days.)

The Cyclorama was so successful that it was imitated. The Panorama, showing scenes of the Battle of Gettysburg, opened on the southwest corner of Seventh and Walnut streets. More of an effort was spent on atmosphere. The ceiling was painted to resemble the sky, and each canvas blended into the next. (The Panorama building was converted into the old Midland Theater, which was razed for the construction of the Grand Opera House in 1891. (This building is still standing, used now as a parking garage.)

Later the Cyclorama became Kellogg's Natatorium, an indoor swimming pool. The ground-floor pool was filled with water from an artesian well in the next lot, which also supplied natural gas. A skating rink was on the building's upper floor.

In May 1886, when a cyclone destroyed much of the Lathrop School on the southwest corner of Eighth and May streets, injured children were brought to the Natatorium. The building that had previously displayed painted scenes of death and destruction now played a real part in a disaster closer to home.

DIME MUSEUM, located in the Hall Building on the northwest corner of Ninth and Walnut streets. The building was razed in 1938 and today a surface parking lot is on the site.
Kansas City, Missouri Public Library - Missouri Valley Special Collections

DIME MUSEUM

The Dime Museum was not like the museums we have come to know. Rather, it was a collection of what some people called curiosities and others called freaks. It was first established in a building on Ninth Street, just east of the New York Life Company Building. Later it would be housed on all floors of the Hall Building on the northwest corner of Ninth and Walnut streets.

For 10 cents the spectator could see many oddities: the Indigo Man whose skin was blue; dwarfs; giants; Siamese twins; the Seven Sutherland Sisters, with yards of hair; the elastic skin man; Millie Christine, the "Two-headed Nightingale" and the two original Wild Men of Borneo — Wayne and Pluto, who were so strong they could pick up and throw men three times their size.

The Dime Museum, operated by Abraham Judah, also presented a man clad in a bearskin coat who gave lectures of his exploration of the Arctic, several tableaux of wax figures depicting atrocities throughout history, and a Punch and Judy show.

Visitors who got through all of this and had another dime could sit down in the first floor theater and see a company of actors perform such plays as "Oliver Twist" or "Lady with a Secret."

The Dime Museum was a popular place. There was no other entertainment in town offering so much. A bargain for 10 cents.

PETTICOAT LANE looking east from Main Street shortly after the First World War. Kansas City, Missouri Public Library - Missouri Valley Special Collections

MAIN STREET looking north from Tenth Street around 1900. Kansas City, Missouri Public Library - Missouri Valley Special Collections

F or the first 70 years of the 20th Century there was a continuity to downtown Kansas City. The majority of the large department stores still bore the names they had in 1900, and many were doing business at their original locations. Office buildings built at the dawn of the century stood side-by-side with the stores. The theaters that presented live performances in the 1880s and '90s had given way to movie theaters, several to a block, whose marquees were a familiar sight on downtown streets. All of these landmarks guided several generations on their trips downtown.

The building of the Sixth Street Trafficway in 1953 was a harbinger of things to come. Construction of this artery, built to move traffic quickly to the east and west, required that 125 buildings be torn down. Although these buildings were north of Sixth or Seventh streets from Holmes Street west to the Intercity Viaduct, many were identified with the business of downtown. Built during the real estate boom of the 1880s, their demolition destroyed whole chapters of the city's history and announced a time of change.

In 1971, demolition came to one of downtown's most important streets, Petticoat Lane, when the 81-year-old Emery, Bird, Thayer Dry-Goods Company building was razed. From the turn of the century until the 1960s, the store had made Petticoat Lane the fashionable shopping street in town. (Although downtown's 11th Street was called Petticoat Lane from the 1890s it was not officially given that title until 1966.)

Petticoat Lane started as a cow path across land that Judge F. A. Smart had purchased in 1857. By the 1870s there were people living on the street, and there was a fruit and vegetable market on the southeast corner of 11th and Walnut streets, where the Mercantile Bank is today.

The city put down wooden sidewalks on the main downtown streets by the mid-1880s, and streetcars started bringing people downtown to shop at the stores along Petticoat Lane, Grand Avenue, Walnut, Main and 12th streets.

Petticoat Lane got its name because the ladies who came to shop, as they stepped off the streetcar would lift their skirts so their hems would not drag in the dust; this would reveal their petticoats. The street became the corridor that channeled shoppers to stores on adjacent streets. Besides Emery, Bird, Thayer, other large department stores opened downtown before the turn of the century. The Jones Store at 12th and Main streets was the only one still in business as the 1990s began.

However, other buildings that used to be department stores still remain. On Main Street at the west end of Petticoat Lane is the building that started as John Taylor's Dry Goods Company. (The business was started in 1881 in a smaller building; the Main Street building was constructed at the turn of the century.) The store was taken over in 1950 by Macy's of New York. Later Dillards of St. Louis would occupy the building, but the company closed the downtown location in 1989.

Peck's department store, on the northwest corner of 11th and Main streets, and Harzfeld's department store, on the southeast corner, have been converted into office buildings. Harzfeld's, a women's and children's clothing store, opened in 1913 and lasted until the 1980s. Peck's dates back to 1866. It started as Doggetts Department Store, one of Kansas City's earliest stores. George B. Peck purchased the store in 1901 and changed the name in 1914. He spent $275,000 to build the store at 11th Street and Main. It was extensively remodeled in 1935 and 1950, then closed in 1965.

People came downtown to shop, go to events at the Municipal Auditorium, attend plays at the Music Hall, go to the movies (the films started at 11 a.m. and ran until midnight), and eat at restaurants. They came downtown to celebrate special events ... the end of a war, Missouri-born Harry S. Truman's election as president, and a welcome for every new year ... attracted crowds to the intersection of 12th Street and Baltimore Avenue.

The decade of the 1980s changed the face of downtown. Former residents who return say they cannot recognize it. With high-rise office buildings and sky walks from multi-level parking lots, downtown has gained a new identity as a business center.

Pictures of downtown streets as they were in the early part of the century may bring back memories. But they also testify to the axiom that nothing stays the same, and today's new structures may be tomorrow's landmarks.

The block of bars on the north side of 12th Street between Central and Wyandotte streets, is now the location of the Allis Plaza Hotel.
Kansas City, Missouri Public Library - Missouri Valley Special Collections

ALLEN'S DRIVE-IN, as it appeared in 1946, when hamburgers were 30 cents and the special Bar-B-Q ribs cost all of 85 cents.
Wilborn & Associates

Behind the FORUM DRIVE-IN can be seen the Casa Loma Apartments, one of several apartments located across Brush Creek, south of the Country Club Plaza.
Wilborn & Associates

DRIVE-INS

A phenomenon of the automotive age was the advent of the drive-in and its contribution to the beginning of the fast-food industry. Many were built in the city in the 1940s.

In 1941, the Forum Drive-In opened at the southwest corner of Ward Parkway and Main Street. The Art Moderne style octagonal structure, owned by Forum Cafeterias of America, Inc., was built by H. H. Fox. Less than two

Bringing bread to the doorstep was a familiar neighborhood sight - the MANOR BAKERY COMPANY'S horse-drawn wagons. They were replaced by trucks in 1951.
Wilborn & Associates

years after the opening it was closed for several months due to the gasoline and food rationing during World War II. It reopened as the Zlan Drive-In — because of wartime meat rationing, New Zealand rabbit was served. From 1949 through 1951 it was the Plaza Nu-Way, and in 1952 it was bought by Sidney's, a local restaurant chain. By 1977, no building was listed on the site in the city directory. An office building stands there now.

Roy & Ray's Drive-In at 4444 Main Street was built before World War II and closed temporarily after the United States joined in the war effort. A sign on the door read: "Roy & Ray have gone to war." By 1972 it, too, had been dropped from the city directory. Twentieth Century Tower occupies the site now.

Dale's Drive-In , 3617 Main Street, was one of several along that thoroughfare. It appeared first in the 1950 city directory as the Valentine Drive-In. Some years later it became Dale's, and its most prominent feature was the large neon sign just west of the carport. Service was available inside as well as at the curb.

Allen's Drive-In, 1418 East 63rd Street (about Tracy Avenue) offered curbside as well as table service in the Art Deco style building. As with many of the drive-ins, hamburgers and soda fountain drinks were the specialities. Surface parking now occupies the site.

Not a drive-in but a drive-out was the Manor Baking Company, which began business in 1926 at 4050 Pennsylvania Avenue in Westport. Stories were told that the basement of the oldest part of the building held a hand-dug well, believed to have been used to supply water for wagon trains preparing to head west on the Santa Fe Trail.

Best known and remembered by many was Manor's home delivery service. When it began, there were 16 horse-drawn wagons. The shrill whistle of the deliveryman alerted residents that he was approaching. The drivers and horses became part of the neighborhood scene. In 1939 trucks were beginning to replace the horse-drawn wagons. The horses held out through World War II and were not completely replaced until 1951. By early 1965, the familiar whistle had stopped sounding in neighborhoods — Manor no longer made home deliveries, becoming instead a wholesale bakery only. The horse-drawn wagons are but a memory.

EDWARD D. DURWOOD RESIDENCE, 5301 Ward Parkway. Destroyed by fire in 1962.   Farnan Foto

DURWOOD RESIDENCE

S tanding atop the hill at the north end of Ward Parkway for more than 12 years was the Sunset Hill residence of Edward D. Durwood, which the owner described as "a poem in natural landscaping." The sprawling one-story stone, glass and redwood house at 5301 Ward Parkway, barely visible from the street, was designed by Jesse F. Lauch, a local architect, in the Prairie style long associated with Frank Lloyd Wright.

The most spectacular feature of the house was a glass cupola that could be reached only by elevator. Durwood called this his "sanctum sanctorum," where he retreated to relax and sunbathe. But the hub of the house was the 25-by-45 foot living room with a projection booth and a movie screen, where movies to be shown in one of Durwood's theaters could be previewed.

Kansas Citians may have known Durwood as the owner of Durwood Theaters Inc., a large chain of motion picture theaters, but years before that he was one of the three Dubinsky Brothers — Maurice, Ed and Barney — entertainers who toured the "Kerosene circuit," playing in every "opry house and shooting gallery," even in tents.

Touring with the Dubinskys was Jeanne Eagels, at the time a chorus girl, dancer and leading lady. Some say Maurice Dubinsky was the only great love of her life. Eagels appeared in the Ziegfeld Follies and gained fame on Broadway and in the films playing Sadie Thompson in Somerset Maugham's "Rain."

While on tour the Dubinskys stayed in a series of closet-like hotel rooms. Ed Durwood, who died in 1961, said that this was why he built such a spacious house. A year after his death a fire of unknown origin destroyed the unoccupied house. Only two chimneys remained, and for many years they were like sentinels on the hilltop. Plans to divide the property into 14 separate lots met with strong neighborhood opposition. Eventually a compromise was reached. Ten lots with eight completed houses known as "Sunset Place" now occupy the site.

The first ELECTRIC PARK was located in the East Bottoms. Built in 1897, the park was dismantled in 1907 to build a second park.
Kansas City, Missouri Public Library - Missouri Valley Special Collections

At night the glow from 100,000 light bulbs that illuminated the second ELECTRIC PARK could be seen for many miles.
Kansas City, Missouri Public Library - Missouri Valley Special Collections

FIRST ELECTRIC PARK
SECOND ELECTRIC PARK

*E*ven the name conjures up something magical in the memories of those who visited Electric Park, or those who were born too late to see it for themselves but have heard about it from their parents and grandparents.

The first Electric Park was in the East Bottoms, near Chestnut and Guinotte avenues. It was built by the Heim brothers - Mike, Ferdinand and Joe - - who wanted to bring more people to their East Bottoms brewery, the largest in town.

The brothers already had spent $96,000 to extend the streetcar line from the City Market to their brewery's front door, but still customers did not come. In 1899, Mike Heim proposed building the largest summer amusement park in the city. It became a showplace and was so successful that in 1901 the brothers sold the streetcar spur they had built for $250,000.

In planning the park, the brothers took full advantage of the newly available electricity — not only to power the rides but to light the area for night-time activities. The Park had one of the first roller coasters in the country, as well as gardens, fountains, and a theater for vaudeville shows. The most famous brass bands of the day, including John Philip Sousa's ensemble, played often for dancing at the Pavilion. But as far as the Heim brothers were concerned, the most important feature was the large beer garden, modeled after those in Germany. A pipeline ran from the brewery to the park to keep the taps flowing.

Electric Park was so popular that special excursion trains brought people to it from all over Missouri and Kansas, and Osage Indians came frequently from their Indian Territory reservations.

As the city expanded southward, the Heim brothers decided to dismantle the park and build a bigger one at 46th Street and The Paseo, beyond the southern city limits. More than 53,000 people came through the gates on opening day, May 19, 1907. At night 100,000 incandescent lights illuminated the 27-acre site, casting a glow over the whole area.

The new park had everything the East Bottoms park had, plus a boardwalk, scenic railroad, bowling alley, balloon ascents and thrilling rides like the popular "Loop-the-Loop." Its pavilion was a popular dancing spot, and the swimming pool was crowded everyday during the summer. Those who saw the large fountain displays remember the nightly shows, waters illuminated by colored lights, and young women dressed in gossamer costumes, who would come out of the fountain as if by magic.

The park flourished until a massive fire in 1925 destroyed many of the buildings. The pool and dance pavilion, spared by the earlier fires, operated until a second fire destroyed them in 1934. For years the rusting skeleton of the roller coaster remained silhouetted against the sky. It was finally dismantled in 1948.

A small city park sits on part of the site of the first Electric Park, and the Village Green Apartments occupy the site of the second one. The Heim Brewery building still stands in the East Bottoms on Guinotte Avenue, as does the boarded-up fire station the brothers built blocks away to protect their first park.

ELKS CLUB building was transported from the 1893 Chicago World's Fair and reconstructed at Seventh Street and Grand Avenue. Today a surface parking lot occupies the site.
Kansas City, Missouri Public Library - Missouri Valley Special Collections

ELKS CLUBHOUSE

*T*he Elks Clubhouse at Seventh Street and Grand Avenue was actually the Wisconsin Pavilion from the 1893 Chicago World's Fair. It was reassembled in Kansas City and was the first building in the nation purchased by a fraternal organization.

Architect Lillian Vaters, a rare woman in the field in the 1890s, designed the building. After the fair, J. C. Rogers, a banker from Wamego, Kansas, bought the building. It was meticulously taken apart and shipped, with blueprints, to Kansas City and put together again at Seventh Street and Grand Avenue. There Rogers opened a private gambling club, The Wisconsin Club — but could not attract enough paying members.

Elks Lodge No. 26, organized in 1884, had been using a room in the New York Life Insurance Company Building for its meetings, but that had become too small for its 300 members. In 1898 the Elks decided to buy the Wisconsin Building; in 1904 they enlarged it to add more lodge rooms and a swimming pool.

By 1934, lodge membership had grown to 1,000 and was preparing for the first national Elks convention to be held in Kansas City. The building was painted a bright yellow in honor of the local lodge's golden anniversary, and because the lodge wanted its clubhouse to stand out so the 35,000 Elks expected in Kansas City that summer would have no problem finding it. (After the celebration the members insisted that the building be repainted a darker color.)

In July 1940, two of the members' wives wrote the Police Department that their husbands were drinking and gambling at the club on Sundays. This prompted several raids. In 1951 the membership decided to move the club to 19 East Armour Boulevard. The old Elks building was sold to the City Union Mission, which replaced the gambling room and bar with Sunday school classrooms.

ELMHURST, more commonly known as the Joseph T. Bird Residence, 3600 Broadway. It was demolished in 1937. The Broadway Valentine Shopping Center occupies the site.   Kansas City Museum, Kansas City, Missouri

ELMHURST

*T*he remnants of a stone wall wrapping around the northeast corner of Valentine Road and Pennsylvania Avenue is all that remains of Elmhurst, an elegant mansion built for John Perry — whose dream for it was never realized.

Perry left England in 1869 to make his fortune. He settled in Fort Scott, Kansas, and went into the coal business, forming the Keith & Perry Coal Company with Richard H. Keith. The company was so successful that Perry and his family moved to Kansas City, where he bought a five-acre tract on the northwest corner of Valentine Road and Broadway.

On the land was a stand of huge elm trees, providing an appropriate name and setting for a rich man's home. It was a stately 18-room native stone house of Southern Colonial style, with a glass-paned cupola. Its architect, Frederick E. Hill, also designed the Edward L. Scarritt residence still standing at 3500 Gladstone Boulevard.

Before the family could enjoy the mansion, tragedy struck. Early in the summer of 1898, as the house neared completion, Mrs. Perry decided to take the couple's four children to Europe for several months. She, 20-year-old twins Sadie and Florence, 11-year-old Albert and 4-year-old Katherine left New York aboard the French liner LaBourgogne. Early in the morning of July 4, 1898, in dense fog off the coast of Nova Scotia, their ship collided with an English freighter. The Perrys were among the more than 600 of the French liner's 800 passengers who were lost.

John Perry and his brother did move into Elmhurst, but only lived there for a year or so. In 1900 John returned to England, where he remarried and lived to age 73.

The house was sold in 1904 to Joseph Taylor Bird, a partner in the Emery, Bird, Thayer Dry-Goods Company. Bird died suddenly on September 9, 1918. His wife, who became known in the business world as Annie R. Bird, was elected president of Emery, Bird, Thayer in 1920. She held that position for many years continuing to live in Elmhurst until her death in 1937. A few months later, in accordance with her wishes, the last and perhaps greatest of the Broadway houses was razed.

EMERY, BIRD, THAYER - DRY GOODS COMPANY faced on three sides, Grand Avenue, Walnut and 11th streets. Built in 1890; demolition was completed in 1973. Kansas City, Missouri Public Library - Missouri Valley Special Collections.

EMERY, BIRD, THAYER DRY-GOODS COMPANY store's arcade along Petticoat Lane was a window shopper's paradise. Kansas City, Missouri Public Library - Missouri Valley Special Collections

EMERY, BIRD, THAYER DRY-GOODS COMPANY

With the possible exception of the Union Station, there has been no other building in Kansas City that has plucked the emotional strings of its citizenry as much as Emery, Bird, Thayer.

The business actually began in 1863, when Colonel Kersey Coates and William Gillis accepted as payment of a debt from Frank Conant a general store located on the corner of Missouri Avenue and Main Street. The store occupied two floors and employed only four clerks. It had, in the new owners' estimation, the potential for success. It was mercantile history in the making.

Gillis sold his interest almost immediately to Lathrop Bullene of Leavenworth, Kansas. In the first year under the new ownership, the store became the second largest business in the young Town of Kansas. Known as Coates & Bullene, sales rapidly increased when the store began to stock household merchandise along with items demanded by those traveling overland on the trails. A short time later, Coates sold his share to T. B. Bullene, Lathrop's brother. The store then became known as Bullene & Brother.

Sales slumped as the city's economy suffered greatly from the effects of the Civil War. However,

by 1867 an economic recovery was being enjoyed and the store once again began to prosper. A new partner, W. E. Emery, joined the business that year and in 1870, L. T. Moore was made a partner. The store became known as Bullene, Moore, Emery & Company. By 1870 business had increased so much that a larger building was needed. The store moved to a building on Seventh Street between Main and Delaware streets. In 1881, Joseph T. Bird was made a partner, and W. B. Thayer joined the company three years later.

Unable to expand the Seventh Street store to meet its needs, the company decided to build a new building. In 1890 the store made its final move into a four-story building on the north side of 11th Street between Walnut Street and Grand Avenue. The design had been executed by Van Brunt & Howe, architects who in 1888 had designed the George Blossom House at 1032 Pennsylvania Avenue.

T. B. Bullene died in 1894 and the store's name was changed to Emery, Bird, Thayer Company. A year later the firm was incorporated as Emery, Bird, Thayer Dry-Goods Company. Under Bird's keen business sense and farsightedness, the store truly prospered. In 1900 an addition was built on the north side, giving the store six stories plus a basement for retail space.

The most well-known exterior feature was the arcade, 562 feet

long and seven feet wide which provided reasonable protection for window shoppers. To enhance the building's interior, over 70,000 yards of carpet covered the floors. From the Walnut Street entrance shoppers could reach a post office branch, the soda fountain or purchase a pair of puttees. Shoppers entering off Grand Avenue would have seen displays of feather and chiffon boas, jabots and mourning veils.

Probably one of the most beloved features of the store was the Tea Room. Located on the third floor, it had opened in 1893. The teas that were served were shipped from Boston and then blended to Mr. Bird's taste satisfaction. For many years, shopping was an all-day affair, almost a social event, with a mid-day break for lunch or an afternoon respite for tea. But with the advent of the automobile and a faster pace of life, shopping became running an errand rather than a day's pastime. Tea Room business suffered and, much to the sorrow of many, it closed in 1941. It was the end of an era. Later the same year a new, more contemporary eating place called the Patio opened in its place.

Also revered was the bank of clocks located above the main elevators on the first floor. They provided the time for various parts of the world. (Shortly after the December 7, 1941, bombing of Pearl Harbor, public sentiment was

such that the Tokyo clock was changed to another city.)

In the 1930s, Emery, Bird, Thayer made legal history. The company challenged a land-lease agreement with the Boston Ground Rent Trust Company that stated the $6,000 quarterly lease payments could be demanded in gold — which by December 19, 1933, would have exceeded $10,000. There were suits and counter-suits until November 1939, when a ruling by the United States Court of Appeals in Kansas City (with Judges Kimbrough Stone, John B. Sanborn and Seth Thomas) ruled in favor of Emery, Bird, Thayer. That set a precedent for other property contracts across the country bound by the same "gold clause." The Boston company lost an appeal to the United States Supreme Court in 1940.

Emery, Bird, Thayer was purchased by Scruggs-Vandervoort-Barney, Inc. of St. Louis in 1945. Hometown ownership was no more. In the battle of downtown vs. suburbia shopping the venerable old store was the loser. It was closed in 1968.

The store was demolished in 1973, ending the long and illustrious reign of the queen of Petticoat Lane. The United Missouri Bank of Kansas City occupies the site.

EMPRESS THEATER 1120-24 McGee Street. Built 1909; razed in the mid-1940s. Today there is a multi-level parking lot on the site. Kansas City, Missouri Public Library - Missouri Valley Special Collections

EMPRESS THEATER

The Empress Theater was touted as the safest theater in the country. Built for the Sullivan-Considine Vaudeville circuit at a cost of $180,000, the theater was designed by the city's leading theater architect, Carl Boller, and built by Halpin and Moore. Constructed entirely of steel and concrete, it was equipped with every safety device available. There were four exits to the alley in the rear, and the entire front along McGee Street could be thrown open to let the audience exit in case of an emergency.

The 12th Street entrance led to an ornate lobby. The interior was decorated in white and gold. There were six boxes and 12 loges in front of the balcony. Fresh, cool air was provided by a plant in the basement that passed the air through water, where it was thoroughly filtered and returned to the auditorium. Dozens of electric fans placed on the auditorium walls also helped keep the theater cool during the summer months.

Architect Louis S. Curtiss, whose apartment was in the building next door, had a door cut from his apartment directly into a box at the Empress so that he could, at any time, slip in and watch the show.

For a time the Empress presented the best in vaudeville and silent movies. Then, with the decline of vaudeville, it became a burlesque theater. It went downhill until the vulgarity of its acts attracted the attention of the police. The Empress closed in 1929, but its owners were caught up in a lawsuit over a 99-year lease the original owners had signed. The legal battle lasted 14 years, almost as long as the theater had been in business.

*FEDERAL BUILDING, CUSTOM HOUSE AND COURTS BUILDING 911 Walnut
Street, opened in 1884 amid controversy around the promised town clock that was
to be in the building. After a new building was built in 1900 the old Federal
Building was sold to the Fidelity Trust Company for $260,000. This building was
demolished in 1930.*
Kansas City, Missouri Public Library - Missouri Valley Special Collections

FEDERAL BUILDINGS

*O*n a day late in the summer of 1845, a crowd of around 300 waited expectantly at the edge of the Missouri River near Francois Chouteau's warehouse for the side-wheel steamboat Trapper to dock. Aboard the boat was a small sack containing the city's first government mail delivery.

This was more than 200 years after the first American post office was established in Boston in 1639. Supervising Kansas City's mail service was William Miles Chick, the first local postmaster. He died soon after his appointment and was succeeded by his son, W. H. Chick.

The early mail business was transacted along the levee, in the stores of the incumbent postmasters. In March 1873, Colonel Theodore S. Case was appointed postmaster. Great strides were made during his 12 years in office. (Case later wrote one of the city's early histories.) Special delivery service was inaugurated, and postcards were used for the first time. The most significant event was the opening of a new Federal Building in 1884, on the southeast corner of Ninth and Walnut streets.

Completed at a cost of $325,000, the Renaissance style building served as a post office, customs house and federal courthouse. But what attracted the most attention of citizens was the controversy that surrounded the installation of Kansas City's original town clock.

In 1883, Colonel Thomas B. Bullene was authorized to appoint a committee of 20 citizens to raise $3,000 for a town clock. The drive was successful, and on December 31, 1883, the bell for the clock — an usually fine one that had been on display at the Boston Exposition — was hung. At midnight it proclaimed the arrival of the new year, 1884. But delivery of the actual clock was delayed. The citizens were irate when they learned that the money had been diverted for purchasing other material for the building. With Postmaster Case's efforts, the clock finally arrived on October 10, 1885 — and was installed at once.

By the late 1890s it became apparent that the building was too small. On July 1, 1900, a new Federal Building opened on the east side of Grand Avenue between Eighth and Ninth streets.

From 1896 to 1900, at the same time that the new Federal Courts Building and Post Office was being built, there was other significant construction underway in Kansas City. Some of the buildings built during that period are still here: The Public Library at 500 East Ninth Street, designed by Hackney & Smith with Adriance Van Brunt was completed in 1897; in 1896 the Heim brothers, who owned the Heim Brewery in the East Bottoms, built twin residences at 320 and 328 Benton Boulevard, designed by architect Charles A. Smith, and Dr. Generous L. Henderson's home at 1016 The Paseo, designed by Rudolph Markgraf, was completed in 1899.

But the Federal Building, done in Second Renaissance Revival style (also referred to as a classic example of "post office" architecture), was just what the city needed: a handsome and modern structure. At the opening on July 1, 1900, thousands toured the building, admiring the dome most of all. The three-story building was constructed of granite and marble at a cost of over $900,000. The west entrance opened into the rotunda, which was 45 feet in diameter, directly under the dome. The sides of the corridors and lobbies were finished in scagolia, and the floors were of mosaic and marble. The third-floor courtroom had light oak woodwork and was furnished with dark oak desks, tables and chairs. The contrast of the woods was very appealing.

Fortunate were those who saw the building after the gold leaf was applied to the dome in 1902 at a cost of $2,500. Seven years later a thorough cleaning of the dome again revealed the building's beauty. The federal government decided the cost of cleaning the dome was too expensive so it was covered with a coat of brown paint.

Less than five years after the building was opened, it became obvious that additional space was needed. Extensions and additions in 1905, 1921, 1924 provided only temporary relief. In 1938 the Cleveland Wrecking Company was awarded the contract to raze the building in preparation for the construction of a new courts and post office building.

The 1900 FEDERAL BUILDING AND POST OFFICE was erected on the east side of Grand Avenue between Eighth and Ninth streets. Locally known as the Customs House, its glittering gold dome was long remembered, even after it had been painted over. The building was razed in 1938. The current Federal Building, designed by Wight & Wight and completed in 1939, is now on the site.
Kansas City, Missouri Public Library - Missouri Valley Special Collections

The mother church of the city's Congregational churches was the FIRST CONGREGATIONAL CHURCH, 1610 Admiral Boulevard. The site is now used by an automotive repair company.
Kansas City, Missouri Public Library - Missouri Valley Special Collections

FIRST CONGREGATIONAL CHURCH

*T*he Reverend Leavitt Bartlett organized the First Congregational Church — the ninth church to be founded in town — in 1866 in the home of W. P. Whelen on McGee Street, just north of 11th Street. By then, the city limits had been extended south to 20th Street and east to Lydia Avenue. There were few sidewalks, the mud in the streets sometimes was knee-deep, lanterns provided the only light at night and wagon trains were still heading west.

For more than 35 years the congregation worshiped in a frame building on the southwest corner of 10th Street and Grand Avenue. It prospered until the financial panic that swept the nation in 1873, during the second term of President Ulysses S. Grant. By 1882 the congregation had recovered sufficiently to buy the northeast corner of 11th and McGee streets, where the Reverend Henry Hopkins dedicated a new church building December 7, 1884.

By 1900, the neighborhood had begun changing character and attendance at the church decreased as members moved away. Two years later, Hopkins had resigned and the Reverend James W. Fifield had become pastor. Fifield was convinced the church should remain where it was and change to meet the needs of the new neighbors. When the church board refused to approve his recommendations, Fifield resigned in 1904.

In December 1905 the congregation decided to buy a site at Admiral Boulevard and Highland Avenue. The Gothic Revival style building erected there was constructed of limestone trimmed with cut Carthage stone. Parapet walls, tracery windows and a massive tower 40 feet square and 100 feet high were much in the English Gothic style tradition. It opened on March 1, 1908. In 1914 a committee of local architects voted the building one of the three most beautiful houses of worship in the city. The other two were the Temple B'nai Jehudah at Linwood Boulevard and Flora Avenue, and the Independence Boulevard Christian Church at Independence Avenue and Gladstone Boulevard.

Dr. James W. Fifield, pastor from 1902 - 1904 of the FIRST CONGREGATIONAL CHURCH when it was located on the northeast corner of 11th and McGee streets, remained for his lifetime pastor emeritus.
Hoffman, photographer (Chicago)

No picture exists of Frank's Hall on the northeast corner of Fifth and Main streets. Tom Thumb, shown here with his discoverer, P. T. Barnum, gave a memorable performance at the hall in 1864. A fire destroyed the hall in 1878.
Kansas City, Missouri Public Library - Missouri Valley Special Collections

In early days steamboats brought entertainment to town. These boats had orchestras aboard and citizens were invited to dances, a welcome bit of sociality and culture.
Kansas City, Missouri Public Library — Missouri Valley Special Collections

*T*he early settlers focused their energies first on shelter, food and moving to higher ground on the south bank of the Missouri River to escape the floods. Their next priority appears to have been entertainment. Joe and Peter Rivard, who came with the Francois Chouteau family to build a trading station, were the settlement's fiddlers. They provided the music for dances during the winter months when traveling was limited and parties were held at the French settlement. There is an argument on who received the first piano in Kansas City, but Berenice Chouteau ordered one from St. Louis bringing culture to the trading station.

The steamboats docking at the levee at the end of Grand Avenue brought circuses as early as 1853. They presented their attractions on board, while the audience sat on the river's bank. The first advertisement for an amusement was printed in the *Kansas City Enterprise* on May 31, 1856, for Mabie's Menagerie and Circus, staged in a tent at what is now 15th and Chestnut streets.

In 1858 architect Percival Gaugh designed a building for Charles Lockridge on the east side of Main Street between Fifth and Sixth streets. Public events were held in Lockridge Hall's second floor. This was Kansas City's first performance hall. It was built over a public sewer, and two years later, when the underground sewer settled several feet, the building was abandoned.

Six halls for public gatherings were listed in the 1860 City Directory. These were spaces above saloons and stores. During the Civil War these halls closed, since people did not want to go out at night and money was tight. Long's Hall opened in 1863 above a bakery and saloon on Main Street, between Fifth and Sixth streets. It was the only public hall in town until 1867, when Frank's Hall opened on the second floor of a building on the northwest corner of Fifth and Main streets.

Frank's Hall had a small, primitive stage, no seats, no dressing room, and the only entrance was a stairway at the rear of the building. But theatrical troupes, lecturers and other performers traveling from St. Louis to California, stopped over and attracted audiences who apparently were starved for entertainment.

In 1864, Tom Thumb, the 40-inch-tall star of P. T. Barnum's circus, appeared there. Thumb was carried into the hall on an aide's shoulders. As the eager crowd pushed forward to get a better look at him, the diminutive performer, afraid of being crushed, let go with a tirade of profanity. That parted the crowd — and was long remembered by everyone who heard it. There were many other performers and attractions presented at Frank's Hall including Ralph Waldo Emerson, author and philosopher, who lectured there in 1867.

Frank's was the best the town had to offer until the Coates Opera House opened in 1870. That theater attracted the better performers and audiences, and soon Frank's Hall closed. The building was destroyed by fire in 1878. The space serves as parking for the City Market.

GARDEN THEATER, the southeast corner of 13th and McGee streets. Built 1911; demolished 1930. Today the land is used for a surface parking lot.
Native Sons Collection

GARDEN THEATER

A rchitect Carl Boller was a popular theater designer in Kansas City before World War I. In 1911, Edward P. Churchill challenged him to come up with a different design for his Garden Theater at 13th and McGee streets. Although the outside of the $125,000 brick, concrete and steel building looked like other theaters in the city, the interior broke with tradition.

Boller's design gave the audience the feeling that it was in an outdoor garden. The walls were of dark red pressed brick, looking like a building's exterior. The ceiling, light blue and curved to resemble the sky, was painted with banks of clouds, and tiny pinpoints of "starlight" twinkled among them.

The lobby looked like a rustic courtyard, surrounded by trellises of blossoms, with brick floors designed to resemble garden paths. On the walls were "windows" with awnings and shutters behind which a glow of light was seen and old-fashioned lanterns were over the doors. The boxes on each side of the proscenium arch were little Venetian houses with balconies and red-tiled roofs. Throughout the theater, over 100 Oriental rugs were displayed. The ornamental ironwork and wooden railings were painted green giving a further out-of-doors feeling.

The Marcus Loew Company of New York purchased the theater in 1919. It was remodeled at the cost of $100,000, and all the original garden effect was eliminated. The walls and ceiling were painted white and gold, and bright scarlet draperies were used as stage curtains. It was now a traditional theater interior.

*JANE HAYES GATES TRAINING SCHOOL,
1920 Independence Avenue, as it
appeared in 1880. It was demolished in
1971. St. John the Baptist Catholic
Church and School occupy the site.*
Jackson County Historical Society.

*JEMUEL CLINTON GATES (1829 -
1915), gave a tract of land at the north
corner of Independence and Highland
avenues dedicated "for all time for the
use of Mercy Hospital."*
Kansas City, Missouri Public Library -
Missouri Valley Special Collections.

JANE HAYES GATES TRAINING SCHOOL

W hile boys took classes in the trades at Lathrop School, girls were learning womanly crafts at the Jane Hayes Gates Training School, thanks to the generosity of Jemuel C. Gates. He had arrived in Kansas City in 1866, a year after the first railroad line had come into the city. With W. W. Kendall, he formed a partnership, Gates & Kendall, and they opened a boot and shoe factory. They remained partners until 1879, then Gates went into real estate making another fortune.

His wealth was such that he built a mansion at 1920 Independence Avenue, a Queen Anne style showplace. Of particular beauty was the hand carved interior woodwork.

Gates died in 1915, five months after he had given a large piece of property for the building of Children's Mercy Hospital. There was one condition of the gift: A plaque honoring the memory of his daughter, Lulie Adeline Gates, was to be installed in the hospital lobby.

Gates' will read that his mansion was to be used as a girls' school for the teaching of home economics and was to be named in memory of his wife, who had died several years earlier.

The school opened in 1916 when the world was in conflict. The Lusitania had been sunk the previous year by a German submarine, with the loss of American lives. The United States was expected to go to war, and did the following year. Along with the regular classes of dressmaking, millinery, and cooking, the students rallied to the war effort. As happened in many schools at the time, students at Gates rolled bandages by the hundreds and sent them overseas. The school remained open until 1938. Until the building was demolished in 1971 it was used by a number of community organizations for meetings and programs.

*GENERAL TIRE COMPANY BUILDING,
1500 Baltimore Avenue, displayed
intricate exterior detailing that
included geometric motifs associated
with the Art Deco Style.*
Landmarks Commission of Kansas City,
Missouri

GENERAL TIRE COMPANY BUILDING

"*H* ere we go again. One of the best-looking buildings Downtown, the old General Tire & Rubber Company building at 1500 Baltimore probably will be torn down in the name of urban redevelopment." So wrote Donald Hoffman, former art and architecture critic for *The Kansas City Star,* on November 21, 1985. It was demolished three years later.

The building was built in 1928 for the Akron, Ohio-based tire and rubber company. For many years the General Tire & Rubber Company was a leader in the field for technical and engineering innovations, including the early production of pneumatic and low-pressure tires for trucks. Kansas City served as a four-state distribution center.

The building, faced with Bedford limestone, was an early example of Art Deco style in the downtown area. It was a significant example of the work of the architectural firm of Greenbaum, Hardy & Schumacher, which a year later designed the Keneseth Israel-Beth Shalom Synagogue at 3400 The Paseo.

Taking its name from the 1925 Paris Exposition International des Arts Decoratifs et Industriels Modernes, the Art Deco style was widely used in the late 1920s and early 1930s. The Art Deco design was also used for the Kansas City Power & Light Company Building, 1330 Baltimore Avenue (1931), designed by Hoit, Price & Barnes, and City Hall, 414 East 12th Street (1937), designed by Wight & Wight.

The General Tire Company Building was in the wrong place at the wrong time, caught in the downtown building boom. It was demolished in 1988. The site remains unused.

GOETZ BREWING COMPANY started on Mulberry Street in the West Bottoms.
Kansas City, Missouri Public Library - Missouri Valley Special Collections

GOETZ BREWING COMPANY later built a large brewery at 17th Street and Indiana Avenue.
Kansas City, Missouri Public Library - Missouri Valley Special Collections

GOETZ BREWERY

*K*ansas City, with its many natural springs and central location in the corn and wheat belt, was a good place for brewmasters to practice their trade. In 1850, Peter Schitgebel's Kansas City Brewery at Third Street, east of Grand Avenue, advertised "The best Lager Beer made west of St. Louis."

In 1863 the Muhlshuster Brewery constructed a large brick building at 20th Street and Grand Avenue. By 1873 there was a "beer depot" at 10th and Mulberry streets in the West Bottoms near the Union Depot. Advertisements said the beer was shipped west on trains equipped with "patented refrigeration cars lined with galvanized iron and packed in ice."

By 1879 the Kump Brewery at 14th and Main streets had a six-building complex, including three ice houses. Kump produced 64 barrels a day and the horse-drawn wagons made three trips a day delivering the large wooden barrels to area saloons.

George Muehlebach came from Switzerland and started making saddles in Westport. In 1870, he and his brother, John, purchased the Hurd Brewery at 18th and Main streets. George ran a four-inch pipe from artesian wells on his homestead property at 18th and Central streets, two blocks from the brewery, to use the spring water in the brew. He expanded the old brewery and its Gothic design

earned it the name of "Beer Castle." After his death, his son, George, Jr. took over. He was better known as the owner of the Kansas City Blues baseball team and for building with his brother, Carl, the Muehlebach Hotel at 12th Street and Baltimore Avenue in 1915.

By the 1880s most breweries were located between 18th and 20th streets, McGee and Washington streets. Anheuser Busch came from St. Louis to open an operation at 20th and Walnut streets. It included a brew shop, bottling area, and stables and stalls for their 24 horses and delivery wagons. The Rochester Brewery was on Washington Street between 20th and 21st streets. Lemp Brewing, also from St. Louis, opened a brewery on 20th Street at Central Street, then later between Grand Avenue and McGee Street in a building that still stands.

The Goetz Brewery started at Seventh and Mulberry streets in 1913 and later moved to the old circus grounds at 17th Street and Indiana Avenue. Prohibition closed down most breweries in 1920. Goetz made a near-beer and ginger beer. (It was common knowledge that the near-beer was bottled with an easily removable cap and enough room left in the bottle to put in an ounce of alcohol. Recapped it was sold by speakeasies as "A Shot Beer" for 25 cents.)

After prohibition ended brewing resumed, but production never returned to the level it had been at the turn of the century.

GRAND AVENUE METHODIST CHURCH, on the southeast corner of Ninth Street and Grand Avenue, was razed in 1909. Today the Grand Avenue Temple Office Building occupies the site.
Kansas City, Missouri Public Library - Missouri Valley Special Collections

GRAND AVENUE METHODIST CHURCH

*O*ne night during the severe winter of 1865-66, the Reverend Stephen Griffis met with 35 brave souls in the parlor of one of the houses on the river bluff. The Grand Avenue Society formed at the meeting was the beginning of the congregation of the Grand Avenue Temple and later the Grand Avenue Methodist Church.

For several months afterwards, Griffis led this group of Methodists in services in such places as log cabins and even in Frank's Hall. But the congregation was growing to a size that needed a permanent meeting place. On April 30, 1866, it bought three lots on the southeast corner of Ninth Street and Grand Avenue for $1,000. This was a huge financial undertaking for the congregation, which did not know how it would raise the money necessary to build the church. An unexpected act of generosity inspired the members to action.

One day Aunt Docia, a former slave and one of the four black members of the church, approached Griffis and placed in his hands $1.25. It was her burial money, she told him, but she gave it "to build a church with so I can worship God, who has been so good to old Docia." The rest of the members rose to her generosity

and raised the money they needed. By the end of 1866 the foundation had been laid; the main auditorium was finished in 1869, and the church was dedicated the following year.

The handsome Romanesque style building had rounded arch windows and a stately steeple. It was the pride and joy of the congregation. So many came to hear the sermons of the Reverend J. M. Pierce, who had succeeded Griffis, and to enjoy the glorious organ music that there usually was standing room only for Sunday services. Many visitors staying in downtown hotels and boarding houses also came, and soon it became known as "The Church of the Stranger."

By the turn of the century, downtown's character was changing from residential to commercial. After much debate the trustees realized the value of the site the church occupied. They voted to demolish the building, replace it with a 10-story office tower and erect another church just to the east, fronting on Ninth Street. They hoped the income from the office building would make the church self-supporting.

A sorrowful congregation assembled on Sunday, October 3, 1909, for the final service. Eight days later demolition began.

Builders of the HANNIBAL BRIDGE in
1869: left to right - George Morrison,
Assistant Engineer; Octave Chanute,
Chief Engineer; Joseph Tomlinson,
Superintendent of Superstructure.
Kansas City, Missouri Public Library -
Missouri Valley Special Collections

HANNIBAL BRIDGE

F ew would argue that one of the greatest events in the history of Kansas City was the opening July 3, 1869, of the Hannibal Bridge near the site of today's Broadway Bridge. Designed by Octave Chanute, it was considered his finest achievement.

Chanute was born in Paris in 1832. His father, Joseph Chanute, was a college professor who came to the United States in 1838 and became vice-president of a college in Louisiana. Octave accompanied his father to this country, eventually earning a degree in engineering. In 1863 he became the chief engineer for the Chicago & Alton Railroad. A year later he came to Kansas City, where he worked as a planner and builder of a number of small bridges. His big moment of fame came in 1867 when he was awarded the contract to design and oversee the construction of the first bridge across the Missouri River.

By only a hair's breadth was the bridge built at Kansas City; Leavenworth, Kansas, also avidly sought the bridge. Whichever town won stood to gain tremendous economic benefits, since it would be ensured of the railroad business as they expanded west.

The final decision rested with Colonel Robert T. Van Horn, a former mayor of Kansas City, who had been elected to Congress in 1864. Van Horn, told of the contest between the two towns, conferred with the chairman of the committee on post offices and post roads. He persuaded him to agree to an amendment of a pending federal bill that would award the bridge to Kansas City.

Work on the bridge began in 1867. The problems and difficulties were monumental. There was only one machine shop and a small foundry in town. Special tools had to be designed and then forged.

Each of the seven piers was built of locally quarried limestone. When finished, the piers were 11 feet above the high-water mark of the disastrous flood of 1844. The total height from rock to coping was 89 feet. When completed, the bridge was one mile long. The bridge, built and owned by the Hannibal & Street Joseph Railroad, provided the first direct railroad line to Chicago, a vital connection. It was an investment of out-of-town capital in the future of Kansas City.

On opening day, July 3, 1869, a crowd estimated at 30,000 to 40,000 was on hand to enjoy the fireworks, parades, music and a balloon ascension by H. R. Holman, who lifted off in his hot air balloon near the Gillis House on the levee.

The festivities ended with a banquet at the Broadway Hotel, (later known as the Coates House Hotel) and with a memorable fireworks display. Of particular note was a cake on display in the hotel lobby in the shape of the bridge, 10 feet long and 2 feet wide.

A "new" Hannibal Bridge was built in 1916. It was welcomed by those plying the river, since it crossed the river straight, from bank to bank, instead of the diagonal position of the old bridge, which made navigation under it difficult because of strong currents created as the river deflected off the bridge's supports.

The old bridge was demolished in 1917 by the Union Bridge Company.

HARRIS HOUSE HOTEL, northeast corner of Westport Road and Pennsylvania Avenue, started as a log cabin built in 1833 by the founder of Westport, John McCoy. The land is used today as a parking lot for a bar.
Kansas City, Missouri Public Library - Missouri Valley Special Collections

HARRIS HOUSE HOTEL

In 1833, John McCoy, the founder of West Port (as it was originally known), built a two-story house and store out of logs on the northeast corner of, what is today, Westport Road and Pennsylvania Avenue. In 1848, John Harris would take over the structure, which would become the Harris House Hotel.

In Westport's earlier days, Daniel Yoacham's tavern was well known among travelers going west. Yoacham built the one-story log tavern in 1824 at today's Westport Road and Mill Street. It was a primitive shelter at best, but it was Westport's first hotel. Enlarged later to two stories, the tavern became the center of the community's activities. The Yoacham family was not only host to all who came through Westport — locals met there to deal in land, trade horses and cattle, get married and hold funeral services.

In the 1830s and '40s, Westport was better known than the Town of Kansas situated at the river's edge. The early western migration brought hundreds of settlers overland to this crossover point. Soon an estimated 90,000 Indians would travel through the area as they were moved off their lands for resettlement in Indian Territory. They took the silver that the government had paid them for their land and traded it for food, clothes, powder and lead, saddles and whiskey. Westport was the last stop for Santa Fe freighters crossing over from Independence before traveling over the prairies and mountains into New Mexico territory.

To get his merchandise faster, McCoy in 1838 instructed the riverboats to unload his supplies on the levee at the bottom of Grand Avenue instead of the drop-off point near Independence. The convenience of leaving trade goods at the levee caught on with other merchants, and the origination point of the Santa Fe Trail would switch to the Town of Kansas in the early 1850s and push the town into prosperity.

By the mid-1840s, Westport Road (from Broadway to Mill Street) and Pennsylvania Avenue south had shops selling food, supplies and trade goods, and craftsmen offering to make wagons, their covers and wheels, tents and guns.

Durig this busy time the Yoacham tavern was filled to overflowing. In 1846, Allen McGee took over the McCoy cabin, enlarged it and opened a tavern. In 1848 John Harris bought the tavern. After the original building burned down, it was replaced with a three-story brick hotel.

Harris came to Westport from Kentucky in 1832 and bought 160 acres, paying $1.25 per acre for land bordered today by 34th and 40th streets, Main Street to Gillham Road. He planted orchards and brought slaves to maintain them. Harris built a log house at what is today the northeast corner of 39th Street and Warwick Boulevard. He married Henrietta Simpson. They had seven daughters.

Mrs. Harris, known to be a very religious woman, would not allow dancing in her husband's hotel. However, it was said that her cooking for guests was so superb that it more than made up for the rule. Those who stayed at the hotel were a cross-section of people: Spanish grandees from Santa Fe, New Mexico, wagonmasters, explorers, gold seekers on their way west, and local businessmen who did not have homes of their own.

Several of the Harris daughters were living in the hotel during the Civil War, which virtually stopped all trade and traffic both in Westport and the Town of Kansas. Although Harris sold his hotel in 1864, his name and the building earned their place in Civil War history.

The Battle of Westport, called the Gettysburg of the West, was fought from Independence to south Kansas City, the armies crossing the Blue River and moving west along what today is 63rd Street. The final clash was in the fields of today's Loose Park. The Confederate soldiers were barricaded above Brush Creek and the Northern forces were mustered on the north side of the creek, where the Country Club Plaza now sprawls. The Union Army's headquarters were a mile away in the Harris House Hotel.

On Sunday, October 23, 1864, General Samuel L. Curtis, in charge of the Union forces, directed the fighting in Loose Park from his vantage point on the Harris House Hotel roof. The Union army, joined by local volunteers, pushed across the creek and over the hills onto the battlefield. They turned back the Confederate forces, but at a tremendous cost in lives on both sides.

The Harris House Hotel was torn down in 1922, but the large brick home Harris built in 1855 at Westport Road and Main Street is still a part of Westport. When Harris died in 1874, ownership of the home passed to his son-in-law, Esmond Kearney. In the early part of the 20th Century it was threatened with demolition, but it was saved in the 1920s through the efforts of historical organizations. The house was restored and moved to the southwest corner of 40th Street and Baltimore Avenue. Many years later it was renamed The Harris-Kearney House. The Westport Historical Society owns the home where its offices are located on the first floor.

HEIST BUILDING, 724 Main street, Kansas City's first skyscraper. Built 1888; razed 1954. The Executive Plaza Building is now on this site.
Sketch from The Kansas City Journal Post, Kansas City, Missouri Public Library-Missouri Valley Special Collections

HEIST BUILDING

The Heist Building was Kansas City's first skyscraper. Although the New York Life Company Building, still standing at Ninth Street and Baltimore Avenue, has always been credited with that honor, the Heist Building was completed a year earlier. While it stood only seven stories high at its Main Street entrance, it continued to the west rising to eight stories on Delaware Street. Because each story was higher than average, it was said that the Heist Building was equal in height to the New York Life Insurance Company Building's 10 stories.

George Heist, who built the building, dabbled in real estate and had a large farm south of the city. His wife, the former Amanda Putnam, is said to have been the first woman teacher in Kansas City's public schools. She also was said to have named the street on which their farm was located, Linwood.

Twenty - three year old architect John George Braecklein designed the building with steel carrying joists, steel girders and cast-iron interior columns, all fireproof. In an interview in 1958, shortly before he died at the age of 89, Braecklein said: "Old George Heist traded a team of mules for the property on which the Heist Building was built. After he had the land he borrowed $180,000 on it to put up the building. You can't beat that, can you?"

For many years the Heist Building with its beehive tower was the most ornate and conspicuous building on the Kansas City skyline. Seventh and Main streets was a popular shopping area. At various times the Heist Building's neighbors included early department stores such as the Logan Jones store (today's Jones Store Company); an early Peck's Dry Goods Company; the Emery, Bird, Thayer store, and Woolf Brothers.

The New York Life Insurance Company bought the Heist Building at a trustees' sale just before World War I and renamed it the Manhattan Building. Tenants over the years included the First National Bank, some brokerage offices and the Kansas City Election Commission.

Architect Braecklein visited the demolition site in the mid-1950s. He was proud of his design for the entrance archway and was looking for the keystone to keep as a memento. He failed to find it in the debris.

JESSIE NEWPORT JOHNSON'S mansion at 2118 Independence Boulevard was designed with Romanesque influence. It was razed in 1931. The Central Baptist Church is now on the site. Kansas City, Missouri Public Library - Missouri Valley Special Collections

DAVID T. BEALS lived in a Richardsonian Romanesque style mansion at 2506 Independence Boulevard, now the address of the Northeast Community Center. Kansas City, Missouri Public Library - Missouri Valley Special Collections

INDEPENDENCE AVENUE MANSIONS

When one views Independence Avenue today, lined with filling stations and shops in buildings badly needing repair, it is hard to imagine that in the 1880s and 1890s this street was the fashionable address for the well-to-do.

In the city's early days, people of wealth settled on Quality Hill. But by the 1880s, the *nouveau riche* were moving east, constructing their grand mansions on Independence Avenue from Woodland Avenue to Gladstone Boulevard. (This part of the Avenue was granted the title of Boulevard, the first in Kansas City.) The mansions cost between $75,000 and $150,000 to build, a lot of money at the end of the 19th Century.

Pen and Sunlight Sketches of Kansas City and Environs, a book about Kansas City published in 1892, stated: "Independence Avenue is a boulevard of great beauty and popularity. On either side of this splendid street are residences of magnificence. The visitor is impressed with the spacious grounds surrounding the houses as well as the tasteful architecture. Many of the leading citizens reside on this street, and it is one of the finest in the West."

Merchant princes, bankers, lawyers, physicians and civic leaders built their homes there. One, August R. Meyer, was Kansas City's first Park Board president and was instrumental in implementing the city's parks and boulevard system, still a model for cities throughout the country.

Meyer, who founded Leadville, Colorado, and made his wealth in the mines there, came to the Kansas City area in the 1870s and started a small smelting company in the Argentine district of Kansas City, Kansas. His business became a huge success, employing more than 1,000 men. From his mansion at 2805 Independence Avenue, he would ride horseback around nearby Cliff Drive and later saw that the area's trees and cliffs were preserved as North Terrace Park.

Robert Gillham, builder of the early cable streetcar system, lived at 2106 Independence Avenue. Before R. A. Long built his 70-room mansion (now the Kansas City Museum) on Gladstone Boulevard, he lived on Independence Avenue. Joseph and Harry Loose, founders of what became the Sunshine Biscuit Company, each had a mansion there, as did lumberman John Merrill. Robert Keith, who owned a large furniture store downtown, kept a stable of fine horses in back of his home at Independence Avenue and Olive Street and he rode horseback to his store at Ninth and Main streets every workday.

Others with homes on Independence Avenue included: Colonel Louis H. Waters, a personal friend of Abraham Lincoln; David T. Beals, founder of Union National Bank; Churchill J. White, who started the Commerce Trust Bank; and W. W. Kendall and Jemuel C. Gates, partners in a

shoe factory, who lived side-by-side on the north side of Independence Avenue between Maple Boulevard and Garfield Avenue.

As was the fashion of the times, the homes had ballrooms and libraries, circular driveways approaching covered entryways, and large stables for buggies and teams of horses. Many of the homes had outdoor tennis and croquet courts. There were extensive gardens, with gardeners to tend the flowers. Walls made of stone quarried from nearby Cliff Drive defined the property lines.

A February 1929 article in *The Kansas City Star,* looking back on earlier times, reported: "The houses were dignified, somewhat pompous never more than three to a block. The motto of the day seemed to be, 'Never a straight line if a curve can be used.' Whenever architecturally possible, there were at least two towers and turrets. And around almost every house swept a spacious veranda; each and everyone had a bay window...made of stained glass in which stars and moons, suns and impossible flowers bloomed in scarlets, purples, oranges and greens trailing their brilliant way illuminated by the sunlight by day and house lights by night."

Those who could not afford to build a house on the Boulevard got the social benefit of the address by living in Fountain Place, luxury apartments that took up an entire block on the north side of the street between Lydia and Highland avenues. In 1886, the Bonaventure Hotel, described as a gathering place for the elite, was built on the

southeast corner of Independence and Park avenues. The owners were convinced that the city was going to grow to the east, and for a time this was a fashionable place to stay. Later, the Bonaventure became a family hotel, then an apartment house for those who were living on reduced income. The building came down in the 1950s.

August R. Meyer led the exodus from Independence Avenue. In 1896 he built a German-style brick mansion at 44th Street and Warwick Boulevard (now the administration building for the Kansas City Art Institute). Others soon followed, moving with the social tide to the new exclusive residential areas in Hyde Park, the South Moreland neighborhood, the Rockhill District, and the J. C. Nichols Country Club District.

By the end of World War I the important names had abandoned Independence Boulevard. Fires, time and vandals wrecked the greatest of the mansions and they came down. Three smaller mansions remain. They can be seen on the south side of the street, just west of the Independence Boulevard Christian Church. One, a funeral home, is remodeled beyond any recognition.

The stone walls that traced the mansions' property lines, still visible on the north side of the avenue from Maple Boulevard east to Prospect Avenue, are the only other remnants of the golden days of Independence Boulevard.

The (first) JACKSON COUNTY COURTHOUSE, on the northeast corner of Second and Main streets. The general contractor was W. B. Everhard. The Dowling Brothers did the stone work. Today, railroad tracks cross the property.
Kansas City, Missouri Public Library - Missouri Valley Special Collections

The (second) JACKSON COUNTY COURTHOUSE covered a solid block - Fifth to Sixth streets - Oak to Locust streets. Built 1891-92 ; razed in 1940. The land is now used as the office and parking lot for the Yellow Cab Company.
Kansas City, Missouri Public Library - Missouri Valley Special Collections

*T*he Jackson County Courthouse at 12th and Oak streets is the latest of several buildings to bear that name. The county court's first home in Kansas City was a building intended to be a hotel. In 1868 several prominent businessmen formed a company to build a hotel on the northeast corner of Second and Main streets that would be "better than anything west of the Alleghenies. It will make Kansas City known throughout the country."

Architect Asa Beebe Cross designed a five-story structure with a tower from which guests were to have seen the Missouri River and approaching steamboats. The interior was to be elaborate. Construction began, but within a few months it was seen that the project was too ambitious for the $20,000 raised. The building had reached three stories when the money ran out and the owners could not raise more. So they sold the building to Jackson County for a courthouse, and it was finished to five stories with a large clock tower in the center.

By 1886, Kansas City's population was 129,474. The city limits were 31st Street on the south and Cleveland Avenue to the east. Much of the city was damaged when the 1886 cyclone hit, but the devastation was worse in the oldest part of town — and the Jackson County Courthouse was right in the storm's path.

The cyclone sheared off the tower and the two top floors. Miraculously, only two persons in the courthouse were killed. One, Deputy Sheriff Henry Dougherty left the building but went back for his umbrella and was crushed when the upper floors fell down into the building. Prisoners in the basement jail were unharmed but

terrified. Many of the county's records were blown away or became unreadable because they were rain-soaked. Temporary quarters were set up in the Lockridge Building at Fifth and Main streets.

The court rented the building on the southwest corner of Fourth and Delaware streets for a year and then moved into the former Board of Trade building on the southwest corner of Fifth and Delaware streets. (This building is still standing.) The old courthouse building was patched up and used for a jail.

A bond issue to build a new courthouse was voted on and a Fifth Street site between Oak and Locust streets was suggested. But there was controversy, caused by various county judges voting for

different sites — some of which they owned. Even after the Fifth and Oak Street location received the most votes, dissenters took their challenge to the Supreme Court of Missouri. The result of the vote was upheld and the court moved to Fifth and Oak streets on April 4, 1892. The building was designed by Charles A. Smith and Frank Rea.

People still were unhappy with the massive $200,000 stone building, and for the next 40 years they called it a "firetrap" and a" monstrosity." In 1935 a new courthouse was built on the south side of 12th Street between Oak and Locust streets. There was an abortive effort to turn the old building into a brewery, but it was torn down in 1940.

The force of the cyclone of May 11, 1886, took off the top two floors of the first JACKSON COUNTY COURTHOUSE. Kansas City, Missouri Public Library - Missouri Valley Special Collections

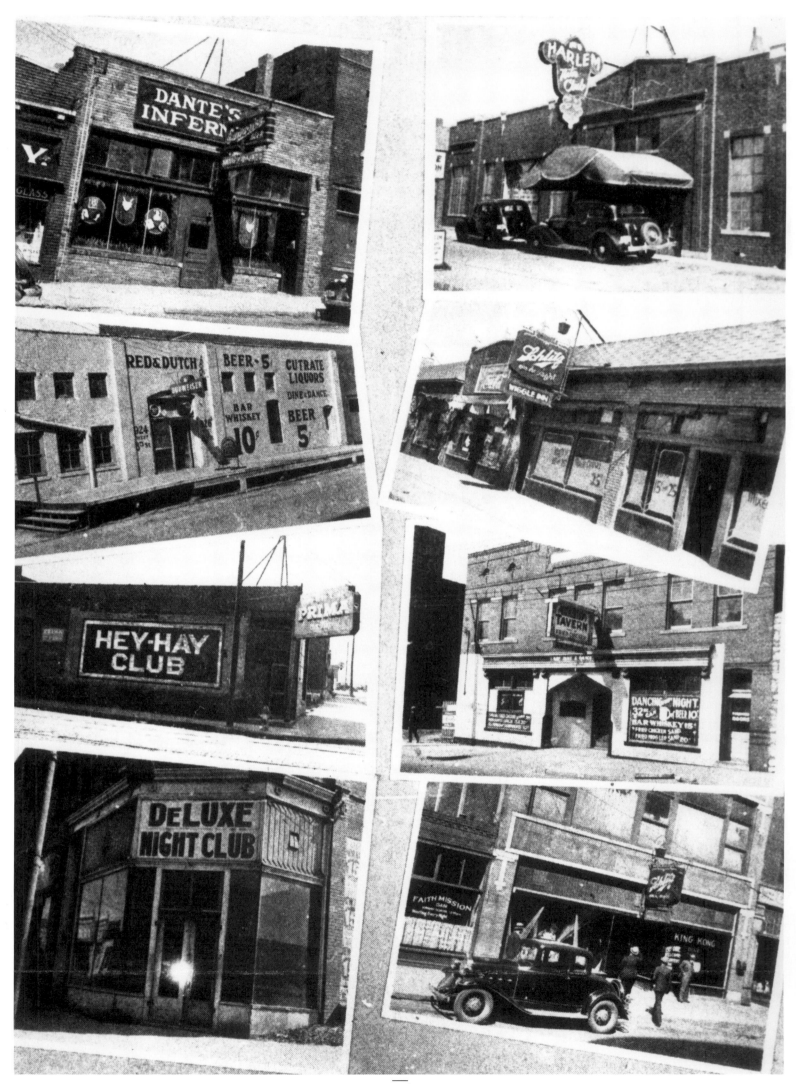

Not before or since has Kansas City exported such a salable product as Kansas City jazz. It began and flourished primarily in an area bounded on the north by 12th Street and on the south by 18th Street. Although Kansas City was not recognized as an important jazz center until well into the 1930s, in the 1920s locals could enjoy the big band sound of that era. The best-known band was the Bennie Moten Orchestra. Then came the 1930s, with Thomas J. Pendergast and prohibition, and the town was thrown wide open. In what was roughly a six-block area, 12th to 18th streets and Highland to Forest avenues, over fifty night spots were opened.

On January 16, 1920 the Eighteenth Amendment to the United States Constitution prohibiting the manufacturing, sale or transportation of intoxicating liquors went into effect. In spite of the law, nightlife went on 24 hours a day, seven days a week. (Prohibition was repealed in December 1933 by the Twenty-first Amendment.)

Clubs opened, clubs closed and clubs moved. It was a transient time, and wherever a door was opened, jazz was played and refined into a style known as Kansas City jazz. Different from either New Orleans or Chicago styles, Kansas City jazz has a distinct two-four beat. Improvisations and more saxophones are used, along with the ever-present background riff. Clubs included Amos 'n' Andy, 611 East 12th Street, Bar Le Duc at Independence and Troost avenues, and the Hole in the Wall at Independence Avenue and Harrison Street where, at the age of 13, Joe Turner sang the blues. At the Lyric Hall, 18th Street and Forest Avenue, saxophonist George Lee and his sister, Julia Lee, who was a fine blues singer, got their start.

Black shows were booked into Kansas City by the Theater Owners Booking Association (TOBA). The talent booked at the Lincoln Theater at 1334-36 East 18th Street by TOBA was mind-boggling: Gertrude "Ma" Rainey, Bessie Smith and Alberta Hunter, each a blues singer legend.

On the northeast corner of 18th Street and The Paseo was the Street Hotel, owned and operated by Reuben Street. The hotel was famous for its Blue Room Cocktail Lounge. Bennie Moten played the Blue Room, as did Harlan Leonard and his Kansas City Rockets.

Below the cocktail lounge was the Subway Club, a cabaret operated by Piney Brown and Felix Payne, a friend of Pendergast. Name musicians who came to Kansas City would go to the Subway to jam. The Dorsey Brothers, Gene Krupa, and Benny Goodman were but a few.

Dante's Inferno — once at 512 East 12th Street , then later at 1104 Independence Avenue — and the Hey Hay Club at Fourth and Cherry streets, also were part of the local jazz era.

Charlie "Bird" Parker, one of the all-time great jazz saxophonists, got his musical start in Kansas City. After graduating from Penn Elementary School he attended Lincoln High School. He left Kansas City for New York to become what many believe to have been the ultimate bebop musician. The "Bird" died in 1955 at only 35. He is buried in Lincoln Cemetery, 8604 East Truman Road.

Not every business in the 18th and Vine area was connected with jazz. The Shannon Building at 1818 East 18th Street housed professionals, doctors and dentists. On the ground floor was the People's Drug Store. On the second floor was the office of the Brotherhood of Sleeping Car Porters, founded by A. Philip Randolph. Also in the building was the Gateway Boxing Club, founded by "Bubbles" Klice. It was not unusual to see boxing champions such as Joe Louis climbing the stairs to the club. And in 1919 the Urban League of Kansas City located there.

Time, blight, absentee ownership and Urban Renewal have taken a terrible toll on the buildings in the area. Many notable structures in the 18th and Vine area were demolished beginning in the late 1970s; The Shannon Building was razed in 1981.

This montage photo shows several early jazz clubs. The HEY-HAY CLUB, one of the popular clubs was located at Fourth and Cherry streets, away from both the 12th and 18th streets of jazz activity. Kansas City Museum - Kansas City, Missouri

KANSAS CITY CLUB, on the northeast corner of 12th and Wyandotte streets. Built 1887; demolished, 1923. Twelve Wyandotte Plaza now occupies the site.
Kansas City, Missouri Public Library - Missouri Valley Special Collections

N ot only is The Kansas City Club, the oldest of its kind in the city but one of the earliest in the West. It was formed in November 1882, in the Tomilson Building on the northeast corner of 11th Street and Broadway.

Members held their first formal reception on the eve of Washington's Birthday in February 1883. However, the Tomilson Building facility was not large enough for the crowd of several hundred people, so the party was held at the old Casino Hall, directly across the street. For protection and effect a canopy was stretched from one door to the other.

By 1885 the membership had grown so large that new quarters were needed. After a careful search, the club bought a site on the northeast corner of 12th and Wyandotte streets for $42,000. The new building was designed by Van Brunt & Howe, architects. The members arranged a loan to build a four-story Romanesque style building, completed in 1887. It had an effect on the club's demeanor: When it moved into the new building, the membership's affinity for gaiety changed. It became staid and dignified. Even political discussions were banned on club property.

From the opening day the club was known for its cuisine. A grill, quite a local novelty, was installed. Members could choose steaks, chops, squab, lobster or frog legs and watch as the chef cooked their meal. The grill room was on the first floor, along with the club's reception room and a barber shop. On the second floor was a billiard and card room and a garden that members enjoyed during the summers. A few sleeping rooms were on the third floor, and the dining room and kitchen on the fourth floor rounded out the facilities. An electric elevator delivered members to the desired floor.

Because the club defaulted on several loan payments, the building was sold at auction in 1898 for $50,000. The membership did not want to move, so the club worked out a lease agreement with the new owner, the New England Mutual Life Insurance Company. Finances improved, and in 1911 the members were able to buy the building for $110,000.

By the end of World War I the club had a membership of 50 and a long waiting list. Another move was necessary. In 1922 the club moved to its present facilities at 13th Street and Baltimore Avenue. The old club was sold to the Stats Hotel Company.

KANSAS CITY COUNTRY CLUB constructed in 1896. Now the site of Loose Park, Mrs. Jacob C. Loose signed a purchase agreement in April of 1927.
                                        Kansas City, Missouri Public Library - Missouri Valley Special Collections

KANSAS CITY COUNTRY CLUB

*A*lmost no evidence remains that Loose Park once was the site of the Kansas City Country Club.

In the early 1890s a number of Hyde Park residents formed the Hyde Park Country Club, gathering for archery, tennis and croquet. Around the middle of the decade, word had come from the East about a game called golf. Several area men decided to find a place to play this new game.

A nine-hole course was laid out in the area where Westport High School now stands, with the ninth hole near 36th Street and Gillham Road, where the home of Katherine Harvey (granddaughter of Fred Harvey, founder of the Harvey Restaurants), would one day be built. It was all very rough — from the start, golfers were beset by cows grazing on the greens. Members petitioned the Westport City Council to enforce the town's herd law to keep the cattle off the course.

The game became so popular that a committee was formed to look for a new site. After a considerable search, they decided on what was the east pasture of the Seth Ward farm, south of today's 51st Street between Wornall Road and Belleview Avenue . (Seth Ward, well-known trapper and Indian trader, built the brick house that still stands at 1032 West 55th Street.) A lease for the 111 acres was signed with Ward's son, Hugh C. Ward.

The club moved to the new course in 1896. A gently sloping drive led up to the stone and frame clubhouse — about where the park shelter now stands. Members arrived by carriage under the east porte-cochere. Before horseless carriages, many arrived by bicycle or on the streetcar to 40th and Main streets, where horse drawn buses completed the trip.

The clubhouse was designed by Walter C. Root, a prominent local architect and a founding member of the club. (Root, with his partner, George M. Siemens, designed the Scarritt Building at 818 Grand Avenue and the Scarritt Arcade at 819 Walnut Street.)

From the clubhouse veranda, members could watch the first tee or look toward the pond (which is still there.) They also could see a swale running diagonally from the southwest to the northeast corners of the property: a bit of the Santa Fe Trail that had been rutted out by hundreds of wagon trains.

The Kansas City Country Club was an immediate success. At first polo was played on the grounds, but members complained that the stables drew too many flies. Hunting and polo enthusiasts, asked to move east across Wornall Road, formed their own club in an existing farmhouse. Golf fever was spreading. In 1897, the Fairmount Golf Club, later known as the Evanston Golf Club, opened in the intercity district east of Kansas City. The Elm Ridge Golf and Country Club followed in 1904 and the Oakwood and Blue Hills Country Clubs opened in 1912.

As the land became more and more valuable, the Ward heirs decided not to renew the club's lease. In 1928 a new clubhouse and golf course opened just off 62nd Street and Indian Lane in Johnson County, Kansas. Several years later, Mrs. Jacob Leander Loose purchased the eastern section of the land for $500,000, giving it to the city for a park in memory of her husband.

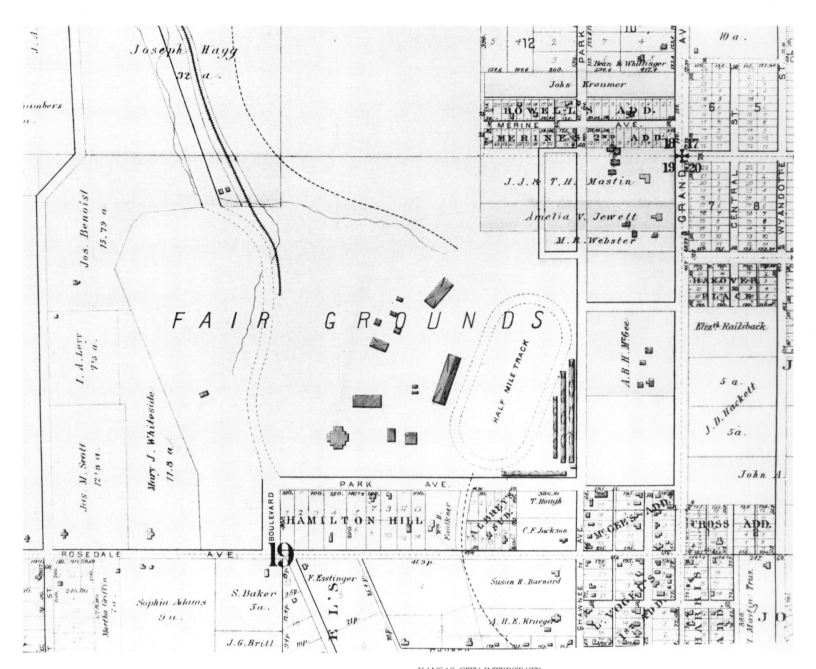

KANSAS CITY INTERSTATE FAIRGROUNDS RACE TRACK was located at what is today Valentine Road and 38th Street, to Roanoke Boulevard and Pennsylvania Avenue. The Valentine and Roanoke Neighborhoods cover the land today. Kansas City, Missouri Public Library - Missouri Valley Special Collections - sketch from The 1886 Kansas City Atlas

KANSAS CITY INTERSTATE FAIRGROUNDS RACE TRACK

*H*orse races began in 1883 on a half-mile track in Westport at the Kansas City Interstate Fairgrounds. A three-deck grandstand faced the track, designed so the lowest seats, 15 feet off the ground, gave a good view of the races without obstruction by spectators at track level. The races were so popular that the stands were packed for the week long event every September for the three years that the track was in existence.

Special trains and steamboats brought people to Kansas City from nearby towns and states to the fair on an excursion rate. To get to the fairgrounds they traveled by wagon, carriages or the Kansas City and Westport Horse Railroad, which left the City Market area every half-hour.

Two hundred horses were entered in races in 1884, and 10,000 spectators came to the fairgrounds to watch the second day of the races. Attendance increased every year, but in 1886 a parade with marching bands and fireworks held in the City Market area, proved competition for the fair. Crowds spent their money in Kansas City instead of Westport. The success of the parade led to the annual Priests of Pallas celebration that entertained city residents and visitors alike for almost 40 years.

The building of the Crystal Palace at 14th Street and Agnes Avenue meant the end of the racetrack. Kansas City merchants were pleased because people attending fairs and races at the Agnes Avenue fairgrounds would be closer to their stores. To attract horse owners to the new site the stakes were set at $10,000 for the winning race. The Westport fairgrounds eventually were sectioned off and sold for residential development. Some people think that the curve Valentine Road makes west of Broadway to the Southwest Trafficway follows the outline of the old track.

KANSAS CITY JOURNAL POST BUILDING

O n October 1, 1855, Colonel Robert Thompson Van Horn bought *The Enterprise*, a newspaper that had been founded the previous year. It went through several name changes and, in 1857 (under new ownership) became *The Western Journal of Commerce*. A year later the name became *The Kansas City Journal,* making its debut as a morning daily.

On March 23, 1865, Van Horn and a partner, A. H. Hallowell, bought back the paper. With renewed vigor, Van Horn assumed charge of the editorial department, where he quickly made known to the public his new Republican loyalty. A staunch Unionist, his allegiance to the Democratic Party came to an abrupt end when the first shots were fired in the Civil War.

Van Horn was very active politically. In 1861, as a Union candidate, he was elected mayor of Kansas City. Shortly after the election he was assigned to a regiment in the Union Army, fighting in the Battle of Shiloh. While serving in the Army, he received word in 1862 that he had been elected to the Missouri Senate. He resigned as mayor to serve in Jefferson City, Missouri. Just two years later he was elected to the United States Senate, serving three non-consecutive terms.

While he was away from Kansas City, the paper carried on. Several moves made room for expansion: to 529 Delaware Street, a new building at 10th and Walnut streets and in 1904, a new brick building at Eighth and McGee streets.

In 1896 *The Journal* was sold to Charles S. Gleed and Hal Gaylord. Following his death, the financially plagued paper was purchased in 1922 by Walter Simpson Dickey. Two years later, Dickey bought *The Kansas City Post* and combined the papers to establish *The Kansas City Journal-Post*.

In July 1922, the paper moved into a building on a site bounded by 22nd and 23rd streets, Gillham Road and Oak Street. It was designed by James Oliver Hogg and was built in 1908 for the Hudson Manufacturing Company, a commercial printing firm.

Extensive interior changes were necessary to accommodate the paper's many departments. Floors required strengthening to bear the weight of the presses and the automatic dispatch conveyers that brought the printed papers from the presses for distribution. Except for Sundays, two papers a day rolled off the modern presses. On the second floor was Alco-Gravure Inc., of New York, which was responsible for *The Journal-Post's* well-remembered Sunday rotogravure section.

Under Dickey's ownership the paper was recognized for its journalistic accomplishments. Dickey, born in Canada, had come to Kansas City in 1885 to join his father, Nathaniel, in the manufacturing of sewer pipes and clay goods. As president of Dickey Clay Manufacturing Company, he amassed a fortune and became active in Republican state politics. President Calvin Coolidge, in Kansas City to attend an American Legion National Convention, once stayed at the Dickey mansion, 5100 Rockhill Road (later, the University of Kansas City's Administration Building.)

The Journal-Post ceased publication on March 31, 1942. For some years after that, the building was used for office and warehouse space. Milgrams Food Company occupied the greatest portion of it. The north Crown Center parking garage is now located on the site.

WILLIAM ROCKHILL NELSON (1841-1915) His passion was to make Kansas City a beautiful city and a worthy rival to all other cities.
Kansas City Museum - Kansas City, Missouri

When THE KANSAS CITY STAR *moved into its new building on the northeast corner of 11th Street and Grand Avenue in 1894, the weekly subscription price was 10 cents. A multi-level parking and office building now occupies the site.*
Kansas City, Missouri Public Library - Missouri Valley Special Collections

THE KANSAS CITY STAR BUILDING

William Rockhill Nelson spent less than two years at Notre Dame University before he decided to pursue a career in law. In 1860 he became a deputy clerk in the circuit court at Fort Wayne, Indiana, then became a lawyer and practiced until the end of the Civil War. He developed a keen interest in politics and was also active in several business ventures. These included, after the war, an investment in a Georgia cotton enterprise. Unknown to him, the company was having financial troubles. Nelson endorsed some notes for his partner, only to have the company fail. Nelson lost his life savings — about $200,000. However, he was able to salvage an interest in *The Fort Wayne Sentinel,* a paper his father had once owned. He credited this as the turning point of his life.

Nelson turned with enthusiasm to his new career as the manager of the paper, and after a year or so he knew that newspaper work was his calling. He sold his interest in the Fort Wayne paper to his partner, Samuel E. Morss, and moved to Kansas City. In 1880, he and Morss founded *The Kansas City Evening Star.* They opened an office at 407-409 Delaware Street, and the first issue appeared on September 18, 1880.

The small amount of capital Nelson had brought from Indiana was soon spent. The paper was successful, but Nelson needed a more efficient press before he could increase the paper's circulation. He approached his friend, Colonel Kersey Coates, who helped Nelson get a $5,000 loan to put a down payment on a new press. Circulation and business immediately increased. In 1889, *The Star* moved into a new building at 804-806 Wyandotte Street. A second press was soon installed that could print about 24,000 eight-page papers an hour.

As circulation continued to increase and a Sunday edition was added (April 29, 1894), more space was needed for press facilities and other departments. Lost time became lost revenue. Nelson wanted equipment capable of printing an entire edition, regardless of size, at the latest possible hour in the shortest length of time.

On October 15, 1894, the newspaper moved to the northwest corner of 11th Street and Grand Avenue. The building, designed by the local architectural firm of Van Brunt & Howe, displayed Second Renaissance Revival influence. Nelson hoped the new structure would provide ample space for a 20-year stay. However, in 1901 he bought *The Kansas City Times.* (Dr. Morrison Munford lost the paper in 1892 when he failed to meet a $100,000 mortgage obligation. A syndicate of Kansas City bankers took control of it, followed by several other owners before it found a permanent ownership by Nelson.)

Within five years, major interior remodeling was needed to make space for the growing departments, but an extra floor and the use of basement space under adjacent buildings still was not enough. In 1908, once again faced with the constraints of space, *The Star* purchased a tract of land on the northeast corner of 18th Street and Grand Avenue for what Nelson hoped would be the paper's permanent home. The Italian Renaissance style building with a stunning facing of tapestry brick was designed by Jarvis Hunt of Chicago. (Hunt also designed Kansas City's Union Station.) Begun in 1909, it was completed and occupied in 1911.

KEITH & PERRY BUILDING, on the southwest corner of Ninth and Walnut streets, designed by Asa Beebe Cross was the pride of downtown in the 1890s.
Kansas City, Missouri Public Library - Missouri Valley Special Collections

KEITH & PERRY BUILDING

*A*ll the tools of the trade — straight razors, shaving creams and shaving mugs could be found in the basement barber shop of the Keith & Perry Building. A wall cupboard displayed an enormous array of shaving mugs complete with the owners' names in gilt lettering. A mug was like a club membership, for it was considered a sign of importance, prosperity and influence.

The six-story building on the southwest corner of Ninth and Walnut streets was completed in 1887 for Richard H. Keith and John Perry (the original owner of Elmhurst, 3600 Broadway), who were partners in a coal and lumber business. The building boasted massive stairways and wide corridors — so wide that they were described as being able to hold a "fair-size" dance with ample room for both the dancers and an orchestra. Open-work, iron grill elevators gave the passengers a sense of ascending in "a captive balloon." The tall, rounded exterior tower was the dominate feature of the main facade. Years later it was referred to as "pigeon headquarters."

Many well-known professional men had their offices in this architecturally significant building — but none so infamous as the occupant of Room 521, Dr. B. Clark Hyde.

On October 3, 1909, Thomas Hunton Swope died at his Independence mansion at 406 Pleasant Street. (Swope had given Kansas City the park land that bears his name.) Dr. Hyde, the husband of Swope's niece, was accused of having administered the philanthropist a fatal dose of cyanide of potassium. Hyde also was accused of poisoning two other members of Swope's family: his cousin, Colonel James Moss Hunton, and his nephew, William Chrisman Swope. All had been Hyde's patients.

The focal point of the trial centered on Hyde's purchase of five-grain cyanide potassium capsules which he testified he had bought to control an infestation of cockroaches in his office. The prosecution introduced testimony by "the most learned entomologists, who never had heard of a cockroach big enough to swallow a five-grain capsule."

Three separate times Hyde stood trial for the deaths. The first trial resulted in a conviction, which was reversed by the Supreme Court of Missouri. The second was declared a mistrial when a juror left the hotel before the trial was completed to be with his bride, and the last one resulted in a hung jury. The state finally dropped the charges.

As happened with so many of the early downtown office buildings, the Keith & Perry Building's useful life ran out. Occupancy dwindled, and in 1946 the Oppenstein Brothers, the owners, planned to demolish the handsome structure to make room for a parking garage. The following year it was granted a reprieve. The tower was removed and for a few years part of the building was occupied by the Union National Bank.

KLINE'S DEPARTMENT STORE was in the middle of the block between 11th and 12th streets on both Walnut and Main streets. A public alley connected the two parts of the store. Both the Main and Walnut street stores were demolished in 1972 to make room for the AT&T Town Pavilion. Wilborn & Associates.

KLINE'S DEPARTMENT STORE

*K*line's department store was in the 1100 block of Walnut and Main streets. To move from one part of the store to the other at street level meant going outside and crossing an alley that ran right through the middle of the store. The alley was not only used by shoppers — it was a short cut for many navigating downtown streets.

E. B. Kline of New York owned Kline's in several cities. The Kansas City store, opened in 1906, was first located at 1125 Main Street in a three-story building and a basement. The store was such a success that in 1909 Kline acquired the Nebraska Clothing Company just to its north, which gave it a 48-foot frontage and an additional four-story building. Sales increased, and three years later Kline's jumped the alley to the east, tearing down the old Globe Theater at 1112 Walnut Street and erecting a five-story building.

The store kept growing. By the mid-1930s, Kline's had the horizontal equivalent of a 20-story building. It had become one of the largest women's wear and speciality stores of its kind in the United States.

By the late 1960s, the declining number of people coming downtown to shop caused a drastic drop in sales. Kline's closed in 1970. As it was being razed two years later, a portion of the building collapsed. The AT&T Town Pavilion now stands on the Kline's site. But every Christmas, Kline's is remembered when the Kansas City Museum recreates the store's tradition of the Christmas Fairy Princess for children of later generations.

LATHROP SCHOOL, southeast corner of Eighth and May streets. Built in 1870. A city horse drawn fire engine responded to the call for help following the deadly cyclone that struck the city on May 11, 1886. Jackson County Historical Society

LATHROP SCHOOL

C yclone and fire struck the Lathrop School in its early years as the 19th Century drew to a close.

The most impressive architectural feature of the two-story red brick schoolhouse was a massive bell tower, which became a deadly force on the morning of May 11, 1886. That day a cyclone roared out of the southwest completely unexpected (this was long before the days of weather alerts.) The storm struck the school and the bell tower, weakened by the wind, plunged with its bell through the roof and the two stories to the basement.

Victims were buried beneath tons of masonry and timber. Fifteen children were crushed to death and many more were injured. Teachers and students rushed to help those who were hurt. Survivors were carried to the Natatorium on the southwest corner of Eighth and May streets, where they were treated by physicians pressed into volunteer service. Rescue efforts were impeded by torrents of rain.

The cyclone continued its deadly northeasterly path, eventually striking the Jackson County Courthouse at Second and Main streets. The tower and the two top floors were blown away, killing two men. Streets flooded, trees were uprooted and houses were destroyed. The city mourned the terrible loss of life.

Soon afterwards, all bells in school towers were removed, and the school board ordered that no other bells be placed in new towers.

Another school — the Powderhouse School at what is now Penn Valley Park, at about 29th Street and Broadway — also was in the path of the cyclone. The winds dislodged rocks from the cliff above the school, sending them plummeting through the roof. Fortunately, none of the 44 pupils was injured. Union forces had built the one-room brick building during the Civil War to protect a cache of gunpowder stored in a cave behind it. (Legend had it that members of Quantrill's Raiders had hidden a quantity of gold in the cave, although none was ever found.) The building was used as a school for only three years, then closed in 1887 and razed a short time later.

Lathrop School re-opened in 1887 at 1214 Central Street, in a new building. On April 4, 1900, it was extensively damaged, without loss of life, by the fire that destroyed Kansas City's first Convention Hall. Again the school was rebuilt, but at the same site. It continued as an elementary school until 1910 when there was an increasing demand for training in the trades — "boys and men in overalls, not in white collars." It was renamed the Lathrop Industrial School, then later the Lathrop Polytechnic Institute, which in 1936 joined the Jane Hayes Gates Training School in merging with Manual Vocational High School.

*LIVESTOCK EXCHANGE BUILDING started as a small house constructed in 1871 at 12th
Street and State Line Road. By 1872 additions had doubled the size of the building.*
Kansas City, Missouri Public Library - Missouri Valley Special Collections

LIVESTOCK EXCHANGE BUILDINGS

A t the end of the Civil War, meat was scarce and expensive in the North and East. Texas cattlemen, who had found it difficult to ship their cattle during the war, had an estimated four million head to sell. By 1867, the Kansas Pacific Railroad (now Union Pacific) had laid track from the Kaw River to as far west as Salina, Kansas.

Joseph McCoy had an idea: Herd the cattle to the rail lines and onto trains that would deliver them to Kansas City. McCoy, called the father of the Kansas City cattle industry, came here after the war from Illinois, where he had a small cattle business. He talked several Kansas City businessmen into financing him, then took a train almost to the end of the line and bought land for one dollar an acre. Within 60 days he had built cattle pens with a capacity for 3,000 head, plus a loading chute, a barn to hold 120 horses and a three-story hotel for drovers. This became Abilene, Kansas.

McCoy hired cowboys to mark a trail for 1,000 miles into Texas, to guide the herds back to Abilene. McCoy's trail was easy to follow. Soon, great herds made it a well-trodden highway from 100 to 200 yards wide. McCoy spread the word among Texas cattlemen that they would be treated right in Abilene. The first shipment from Abilene to Kansas City was made September 1, 1867.

The West Bottoms' yards handled 700,000 head of cattle in 1871. The Kansas City Stockyards Company was incorporated that year on a 13-1/2 acre site on the east bank of the Kaw River near the Kansas Pacific railroad tracks, just south of 12th Street and State Line Road. The yards would grow to cover over 200 acres, second only to Chicago as the receiving and distribution point for this country's meat industry.

The first Livestock Exchange Building, built in 1871, was frame, one and one half stories and 24 feet square, on the Kansas side of the stockyards. The cattle business was growing so rapidly that the building had to be doubled in size before the end of 1872. Two banks had offices in the building, handy to the cattlemen who were paid in gold.

In 1876 a three-story brick exchange building was constructed at 16th Street and State Line Road at a cost of $35,000. Originally 105 by 127 feet in size it was enlarged in 1895 to three and one half acres of floor space with room for 350 offices. By 1909 the livestock business outgrew this building. The present nine-story Livestock Exchange Building at 1600 Genessee Street was completed in 1911.

What happened to Joseph McCoy? He made his investors wealthy. They had promised him a commission on each head of cattle delivered to Kansas City, but he said he never received any money. McCoy later earned his living as a livestock inspector in the yards. He died in 1915 in a cheap rooming house on Broadway. His obituary identified him merely as a "pioneer cattleman."

When the West Bottoms was at the height of the livestock business, each pen was filled with cattle waiting to be processed.
Kansas City, Missouri Public Library - Missouri Valley Special Collections

*MANUAL TRAINING HIGH SCHOOL,
15th Street and Tracy Avenue. When it
opened in 1897 it was heralded as the
first public vocational school in the
United States. Two years of manual
training courses, in addition to the
usual college preparatory work, was
required.*
Kansas City, Missouri Pub.ic Library -
Missouri Valley Special Collections

"People think we're cranks," said Gilbert Morrison. "Of course we're cranks," replied E. D. Phillips. "But what is a crank? It's a handle that turns a wheel. We've got to keep cranking."

With this conviction, Morrison and Phillips, two public high school teachers, tried for five years to convince the public and the Board of Education to try a different kind of high school. Their concept was "to correlate the hand with the brain." They believed the combination of handwork and academic subjects would allow students "to exercise their best powers while obtaining accurate information in many practical matters."

They succeeded, for on September 27, 1897, Manual Training High School opened in a new building at 15th Street and Tracy Avenue. Morrison was principal; he and his hand-picked faculty fretted before school opened about just how this new approach to education would be received. They did not have to worry: hundreds of students surged through the doors, and the opening-day enrollment was 740.

Educators from around and beyond the country came to inspect the program offered in the three-story brick building. Girls in the first cooking class, wearing skirts of such length that only the tips of their shoes showed, were called Miss Manualites. Boys were busy learning about such things as steam and electricity, machine shop work, carpentry and forging. Full college preparatory courses (except Greek) also were part of the school day.

In 1906 the Conservatory of Music was begun at Manual High by J. A. Cowan, a drama teacher at the school. His dream was to make Kansas City the music capital west of the Mississippi River. Over the years it merged with other music schools. Now part of the University of Missouri-Kansas City, it is the oldest operating musical institution in the city.

Manual received two gold medals at the 1904 World's Fair in St. Louis: One was for a display cabinet the students made to hold their illustrated notebooks. The other was a special award to E. D. Phillips for arranging the exhibit.

Manual Training High School closed in 1936 after more than 38 years of classes. The site is occupied by the Metropolitan Advance Technical High School.

People liked to picnic at MILTON McGEE'S farm and visit the animals he kept there.
Kansas City, Missouri Public Library - Missouri Valley Special Collections

MILTON McGEE RESIDENCE

*T*he McGees, one of the most influential families in early Kansas City, owned much of the land that made up the city's core. James Hyatt McGee came here from Kentucky in 1828 and became one of the stockholders in the Town Company, which owned the original townsite that became Kansas City. He purchased vast acreage between Ninth and 23rd streets, Summit Street to Troost Avenue. He built his home, the first brick house in Jackson County, at the northwest corner of 19th and Main streets. His oldest son, Allen, bought land near Westport, opened an outfitting store there for the Santa Fe traders and prospered.

Milton McGee, another son, was to become the best known of the McGees and one of the early city's most flamboyant citizens. He ran away from home when he was 12. At 16, he was fighting Seminole Indians in Florida and later fought Indians in Texas, where he married. He returned with his bride to farm on his father's property. In 1849 he abandoned his wife and farm to join the California Gold Rush, and in 1851, he returned with saddlebags full of gold.

McGee used his riches to buy land stretching from 12th Street to Westport Road and from Main to Holmes streets. He then started a stagecoach line that ran from the Harris House Hotel in Westport to the levee at the Missouri River. He graded and widened Market Street (now Grand Avenue) to accommodate the wagon trains that were on their way to Santa Fe. McGee also built a small home just off Market Street, near 18th Street.

By 1856, seeing that the only hotel in town located at the levee was filled, McGee built additions to his house and turned it into the Wayside Inn — sometimes called the Planters, the Farmers Exchange and the Southern Hotel. McGee, active in the pro-slavery movement, made the hotel a place where Southern emigrants could discuss politics. He would meet steamboats at the levee with a brass band and offer a carriage to transport potential guests to his hotel.

Some considered McGee's land, a mile south of the levee, too far away from the town. In 1857, believing that the town would move southward, he built a row of two-story brick buildings on the east side of Grand Avenue between 13th and 14th streets, calling them the Metropolitan Block. The buildings stood in the middle of a cornfield.

In 1858 he gave Kansas City's first big party, a Fourth of July celebration at McGee's Grove near 15th and Locust streets. Over 3,000 attended to eat barbecue and listen to a brass band.

In 1868 McGee built a two-story Italianate style brick house on his 13-acre farm at what is now 17th and Wyandotte streets. The house had an entrance gate made from a whale's jawbone. Many prominent visitors stayed there. Washington Irving, author of "Rip Van Winkle" who came through on his way to write about the West, stayed with McGee. So did royalty from Germany and England, who had come up the river to hunt buffalo. On Sundays, townspeople picnicked on the grounds where McGee kept a brown bear, a dozen deer, bald eagles, antelope and other wildlife in a five-acre fenced enclosure — Kansas City's first zoo.

In 1870 Milton McGee was elected mayor on the Democratic ticket. He died three years later.

In 1867 MECHANICS BANK built their building on the northwest corner of Second and Main Streets shortly after Main Street was cut through the bluffs behind the levee. Today railroad tracks cross the land.
Kansas City, Missouri Pub.ic Library - Missouri Valley Special Collections

*M*echanics Bank was the city's first bank. Its second building on Main Street also served as the depot for the Santa Fe stagecoach.

The bank was founded in St. Louis in 1857. Nehemiah Holmes (for whom Holmes Street is named), purchased the rights for a branch in Kansas City. It opened on Commercial Street on the riverfront, the levee's main business street.

Soon afterwards, the Kansas City Savings Association, the second bank in town, was built at Third and Delaware streets. The building also housed two insurance companies, a law firm and the Magnolia restaurant. This bank was later rechartered and in 1887 became the National Bank of Commerce.

By 1869 the Mechanics Bank's deposits had grown and it needed a larger building. Holmes chose to build his two-story brick building at Second and Main streets, between the tall bluffs that ran parallel to the riverfront.

The stagecoach depot in the Mechanics Bank Building was a meeting place for freight handlers and passengers. There was a lot of bartering and trading in front of the bank, which added to the deposits. Passengers willing to brave Indian Territory and the mountains to reach Santa Fe, New Mexico, gathered at the building to embark on the 13-day trip. The stagecoach could hold 12 people. The one-way fare was $175 and the stagecoach left at seven a.m. every Saturday.

Adding to the bank's deposits were the shipments of silver and gold sent back by Santa Fe traders. Returning mail coaches carried these shipments for deposit to the Mechanics Bank, later to be transferred aboard guarded steamboats bound for eastern cities.

Even though the bank was a success, when Nehemiah Holmes died, in 1873, the Kansas City branch was absorbed by its parent company and moved to St. Louis.

KANSAS CITY SAVINGS BANK, the city's second bank, built an Italinate building in 1868 at Third and Delaware streets.
Kansas City, Missouri Public Library - Missouri Valley Special Collections

MIDLAND HOTEL at 705 Walnut Street. Built 1888. Today the land is used as a surface parking lot.
Kansas City, Missouri Public Library - Missouri Valley Special Collections

MIDLAND HOTEL

W hen the Midland Hotel opened September 6, 1888, it was acclaimed as Kansas City's first modern hotel and posed a threat to the Coates House Hotel. The Midland was the first to be built equipped with electricity (although gas jets were on the wall, in case of power failure.) It also was the first fireproof hotel in the city. Twelve rooms had private baths, a novelty at the time.

Designed by Burnham & Root of Chicago in the Romanesque style, the seven-story brick hotel had a tunnel-like lobby running from Walnut Street to Main Street. In the center of the hotel, from the second to the seventh floors, was a great spiral staircase with marble steps and wrought-iron railings.

For a time, before the Baltimore Hotel opened, the Midland Hotel played host to all the dignitaries, including Presidents William McKinley, Benjamin Harrison, Grover Cleveland, Theodore Roosevelt and William H. Taft. Admiral George Dewey stayed there, as did all the stars playing at the Auditorium Theater on East Ninth Street and those performing at the Grand Opera House across the street from the hotel on the southwest corner of Seventh and Walnut streets. (The Grand was built on the site of the old Midland Theater, formerly the Panorama House, which displayed floor-to-ceiling scenes of the Battle of Gettysburg, painted on canvas.)

Hotel workers remembered Mrs. John Drew, the actress, was a frequent guest. She often traveled with her young grandson, Lionel Barrymore, later a famous stage and film star.

The Midland Hotel's fifth-floor banquet room was 100 feet long and 50 feet wide, without a pillar to obstruct the view. An orchestra on a balcony in the lobby played nightly for dancing. In the basement were steam baths and a swimming pool. (Men who stayed too long at the lobby bar could go to the steam baths to sweat out the liquor before going home to their families.) The bar and steam baths were particularly appreciated during the 1900 Democratic National Convention when politicians filled the hotel for a week. A senator from Montana chalked up a bill for $3,000 at the long, mirrored bar.

The Midland Hotel was famous as a political headquarters of both the "Goats" and the "Rabbits" factions of the local Democratic Party. (Jim and Tom Pendergast's followers were the "Goats.") They met in the hotel's Parlor S, where they fought it out trying to agree on candidates to beat the Republicans.

Thanksgiving week was lively at the Midland as it was the home-away-from-home for University of Missouri alumni waiting for the results of the annual Kansas-Missouri football game.

When the Baltimore Hotel opened in 1899, its elegant design and luxurious accommodations drew the better clientele away from the Midland. In 1908 the Chicagoans who owned the Midland decided to convert it into offices. It was known as the Midland Building until 1917, when it was purchased by the local railroads and renamed the Railway Exchange Building. Thirty-two railroad companies housed offices in the building.

WILLIAM J. SMITH lived in one of the largest mansions on "Millionaire's Row." He bought the Romanesque style mansion, built in 1890, at 3000 Troost Avenue from George F. Winter. The house was razed in 1938. Wonder Bread Bakery is diagonally across the street.
Kansas City, Missouri Public Library - Missouri Valley Special Collections

WILLIAM J. SMITH was called "Cable Road Smith" because he built Kansas City's first street cable carline down Troost Avenue. His home later became Horner Institute, the beginning of today's University of Missouri-Kansas City Conservatory of Music.
Kansas City, Missouri Public Library - Missouri Valley Special Collections

WILLIAM A. WILSON built his Romanesque style mansion in 1880 at 2700 Troost Avenue. Wilson traveled the world buying furnishings for his home that many said made it look like a museum.
Kansas City, Missouri Public Library - Missouri Valley Special Collections

MILLIONAIRE'S ROW

*T*he name "Millionaire's Row" was given to Troost Avenue from 26th to 32nd streets because of the many wealthy persons living in its mansions. During the 1890s, Troost Avenue rivaled Independence Avenue as the street of mansions. But "Millionaire's Row" had something Independence Avenue did not have... a resident who was one of the richest men in the country. Lamon Vernon Harkness, worth $150 million, built a 12 room brownstone house at 3125 Troost Avenue in 1888. He had inherited his fortune from his father, who had been a partner with John D. Rockefeller in the Standard Oil Company and other ventures.

Harkness did not spend much time at his house. He used his wealth to seek pleasures and traveled the world, then left Kansas City for good in 1891 after acquiring a horse-breeding farm near Lexington, Kentucky.

The development of the 31st Street and Troost Avenue area started with the Reverend James Porter plantation. The Methodist minister came from Tennessee in 1834 with his family and 40 slaves. With a government grant he purchased 365 acres of land at $1.25 per acre from what today is 23rd to 31st streets and Locust Street to The Paseo. This included several springs. Later, water from one near 28th Street and The Paseo would be piped to the Troost Amusement Park to feed the lake there.

Porter built his home at what is now 28th Street and Tracy Avenue, with slave quarters at 27th Street. He would soon have as many as 100 slaves who worked his orchards, corn fields and took care of his cattle. When Porter died in 1851, his land was divided between his children, but it was not until 1886 that the farm was developed for residences. In 1888 George F. Winter, a millionaire, bought the entire block of Troost Avenue between 30th and 31st streets to Harrison Street, building his mansion on the southwest corner of 30th Street and Troost Avenue. (At this time 31st Street was called "Springfield".)

The mansions on Troost Avenue looked much like their counterparts on Independence Avenue. They had several peaked and gabled roofs, towers, and porte-cocheres, the latter giving shelter to the guests arriving at the entranceway.

In 1901 *The New York Herald* published a list of 23 millionaires living in Kansas City. A fourth of them lived on the six blocks of "Millionaire's Row," as did T. T. Crittenden, former mayor of Kansas City and Governor of Missouri; William T. Kemper, founding father of the Commerce Bank; and George B. Peck who owned Peck's Department store downtown.

W. A. Wilson's mansion at 27th Street and Troost Avenue was built in 1880. On his travels, Wilson bought works of art to display in his home. It was finished with Turkish carpets and divans. The bathroom was tiled with Delft tiles and the walls surrounding the carved winding sycamore wood stairway were covered with Oriental silk banners and French tapestries. There were Chinese lacquered cabinets, ebony tables from Africa, and a fireplace with a mantel of Mexican onyx. In the living room was a collection of porcelain vases - Dresden, Sevres and Royal Worchester. Every room was paneled in a different wood, and on the walls were original paintings and excellent copies of "old" masters' works.

One of the most famous mansions on "Millionaire's Row" belonged to William J. Smith. Lamon Harkness may have had more money than other residents, but his house of 12 rooms was small compared with Smith's mansion. He was a partner with Robert Gillham in the Kansas City Cable Railway Company, the first cable streetcars. When Smith sold his stock in the company he became rich and bought the George F. Winter residence on the southwest corner of 30th Street and Troost Avenue for $110,000.

On each of the mansion's three floors was a large hall with a massive fireplace framed in carved mahogany with mantels of onyx and marble. The central stairway leading from the first floor was also of mahogany and had carved posts. The halls were paneled with solid mahogany and ceilings were 14 feet high. Rooms radiated around the hall in a circle, connecting with one another. Each room was finished in a different rare hardwood with cabinets, cases and furniture made of the same wood.

The drawing room on the first floor had panels and frames of satinwood, and there was gold hardware on all the doors and windows. The ceiling had been copied from a palace at Fontainebleau. The first-floor library held 2,000 books, one of the finest private collections in Kansas City. The entire house was carpeted.

There were six daughters and two sons in the Smith family, and they entertained often. The dining room table could easily seat 24 and the kitchen was as large as most hotel kitchens. There were parties almost every weekend. On the third floor were two ballrooms plus billiards rooms, ping-pong rooms and an entrance to a large porch. In the basement were bowling alleys.

In the winter the house was kept warm by a heating plant in the basement of the stable. Heated air was pumped through a tunnel in the cold months and fresh air cooled as it went through the tunnel was pumped through the house in warm weather. It was probably the first house in the city to have air-conditioning.

"Millionaire's Row," like Independence Avenue, ceased to be a desirable address for the wealthy around World War I. There is no evidence of the mansions now.

T. T. CRITTENDEN, former Missouri Governor and Mayor of Kansas City, lived on the southeast corner of 26th Street and Troost Avenue. He was appointed by President Grover Cleveland to be Consul General to Mexico.
Kansas City, Missouri Public Library - Missouri Valley Special Collections

"The Jazz Singer," the first "talkie" was shown at the GLOBE THEATER built in 1913 on the southwest corner of 13th and Walnut streets.
The Kansas City Star

The interior of the NEWMAN THEATER.
Herb Simon

MOVIE THEATERS

In 1897, three early silent films, each 50 feet long, were presented by the French Lumiere Cinematograph Company at the Coates Opera House. The subjects of the film were: the Grand Canal of Venice; the Black Diamond Express, showing a fast-moving train that made people jump from their seats, expecting the train to run over them; and the controversial "Kissing Duet," in which John Rice and May Irvin embraced and kissed — the first movie love scene.

A year earlier, Kansas City resident George W. Curtis became interested in filming and obtained a motion picture camera using a process called animatography. With a friend, Curtis went to Ninth and Main streets and filmed cablecars going through the intersection and other Kansas City street scenes, including a horse-drawn fire wagon on the way to a fire. These early Kansas City films are preserved at the Kansas City Museum.

By 1898 the Orpheum Theater at Ninth and May streets was showing films made by the American Biograph Company between vaudeville acts. In 1901, Carl Mensing (owner of "Yales Electric Exposition," a penny arcade at 720 Main Street), partitioned off the back room and hung a sort of screen on which images of film were cast by a dim lantern. He called it the Mutoscope Parlor and it was the first place that showed motion pictures on a regular basis. Other makeshift theaters opened, including one in the East Bottom's Electric Park.

By 1910 there were nearly 100 motion picture theaters in Kansas City. According to an article in the June 28, 1910 *Kansas City Journal*, parents were complaining about the effects of motion pictures on their children's eyes. They also thought it promoted juvenile delinquency and made it difficult for poor parents to deny money to

their children to attend the movies.

As movies became more sophisticated, the small room theaters disappeared and the grand movie palaces were built downtown.

The Globe Theater is where Kansas Citians saw their first talking motion picture: "The Jazz Singer" in 1927. In this first talkie, Al Jolson was heard singing, talking and weeping. The film revolutionized the industry.

There were two Globe Theaters. The first one was on the east side of Walnut Street between 11th and 12th streets where Kline's department store was later built.

The second Globe, built in 1913, was on the southwest corner of 13th and Walnut streets and was owned and operated by the Oppenstein Brothers. The 2,000 seat theater presented both vaudeville and photoplays (films). Constructed of reinforced concrete and steel, it was made to last but

only stood for 19 years. It included two innovative design features. All of the inside supporting posts were eliminated so that nothing obstructed the audience's view, and the electrician's booth was suspended outside the theater proper — a great precaution against fire.

An interesting feature at the Globe was an animal room. Because many of the touring vaudeville acts had performing dogs, monkeys, and seals, the Globe had a room especially for them including a swimming pool for the seals. The room was said to be odor proof.

As vaudeville waned, the Globe turned more to films. To compete with other downtown theaters, the Globe installed a $15,000 pipe organ in 1923 to play during silent films. But it was "The Jazz Singer" that really sold tickets. People waited in line for blocks to get in. That success was short-lived

LIBERTY THEATER at 1104-06 Main Street was built in 1918. In the 1940s it was renamed the Roxy after a popular New York Theater. It was torn down in 1974 for the construction of City Center Square.
Kansas City, Missouri Public Library - Missouri Valley Special Collections

LIBERTY THEATER'S interior was decorated in the grand style of early movie palaces.
Kansas City, Missouri Public Library - Missouri Valley Special Collections

however. By 1930, the Globe had closed, and in 1932 the decision was made to tear the building down. The wrecking company was paid only $1,000, but it got the pipe organ, the 2,000 seats, all of the steel in the building and the exterior terra cotta bricks.

The owners said the land would be used "temporarily" as a parking lot. It remains a parking lot today.

The Liberty and Newman Theaters stood near each other on the west side of Main Street between 11th and 12th streets. The names of both were changed and both were torn down at the same time.

The name "Liberty" was first given to a theater on Southwest Boulevard. The second Liberty would survive until the 1970s as the Roxy Theater.

Frank Newman was hailed as a builder of opulent theaters in Kansas City. He first built the Royal Theater at 1022 Main Street in 1914. It was called the forerunner of the grand downtown movie palaces.

The Newman Theater opened in 1918 at a cost of $400,000; the largest theater in downtown at the time. A colonnade went across the upper facade and there was marble used throughout the interior. Although it opened as a movie theater, the Newman was built with a stage that could accommodate live performances, and it had a large orchestra pit.

Downtown was primarily a business district, and merchants worried that theaters, taking people off the streets and away from display windows for two hours, would hurt sales. But more theaters opened, bringing more people downtown.

In 1924 there was a demonstration of "Phonofilms" at the

Newman Theater. The system was invented by Lee DeForest, who imprinted sound onto the celluloid along with the film's action. After the demonstration *The Kansas City Star* said: "Like every other pioneer project, there are great improvements to be made in the development of the new-type film ... perhaps the most needed at present is in the development of a better type of loud speaker for the reproduction of the voice and music." It would take Hollywood three more years to improve sound technology.

In 1925 Frank Newman sold both the Royal and Newman to the Los Angeles-based Famous Player/ Lasky Films (later Paramount) for $900,000. The Newman became the home of Paramount and Warner Brothers pictures in Kansas City. (Each of the big downtown theaters had exclusive rights to show first runs of the films of one or two major studios. The Tower

Theater played 20th Century Fox films. The Loew's Midland showed MGM movies, RKO products were shown at the Orpheum and the Esquire was the home of Universal Studio films.)

In the 1950s the Newman was renamed the Paramount. Then in the 1960s the theater was remodeled into four theaters and given the name "Towne" but later renamed the Paramount. Both the Roxy (the renamed Liberty Theater) and the Paramount were razed in the mid-1970s to make way for City Center Square.

The Pantages Theater was on the south side of 12th Street just west of McGee Street. Its ornate Renaissance style reflected the times when theaters were designed to look like palaces. It cost $900,000 to construct. The theater was the 33rd built by Alexander

Pantages, who wanted a theater in all the major United States cities. It was built as a vaudeville house.

The theater seated 2,200, and its distinctive 180 foot tower at the entrance on 12th Street could be seen all over downtown. At the tower's pinnacle was a revolving lighted sign that spelled out "Pantages." There were no supports or beams in the audience portion, so the stage was visible from every seat. The ceiling had a stained glass dome, and the interior was finished in bronze.

The public flocked to the new theater at first, but as other theater owners learned, the public could be fickle. By 1930 the theater had changed hands and was showing movies along with vaudeville. It closed for awhile and reopened as the Tower Theater.

The Tower was the city's last theater to present vaudeville.

PANTAGES THEATER later the TOWER, at 213 East 12th Street. Built in 1921, it was designed by P. M. Priteca of Seattle, Washington.
Kansas City, Missouri Public Library - Missouri Valley Special Collections

Performers on their way up as well as those on their way down played the Tower. The theater had a master of ceremonies and its own dancers - "The Tower-A-Dorables" and presented vaudeville acts along with first-run movies. In 1939, Walt Disney's "Snow White and the Seven Dwarfs" filled the seats but the theater's survival was touch and go.

In the 1960s the Tower's screen and equipment were converted to show Mike Todd's Cinerama production of "Around the World in 80 Days." Crowds came to see the new marvel, and for a short time, the Tower again was popular. When the film closed, so did the Tower. Now the site is just another parking lot.

Kansas City not only had its share of movie theaters but it was a distribution point for films throughout the Midwest. In 1921 large movie companies started locating offices in the city concentrating in the vicinity of Wyandotte Street and Baltimore Avenue, between 17th and 18th streets. The area was called "Film Row." Metro-Goldwyn-Mayer, Warner Brothers, 20th Century Fox, Paramount, Universal, as well as smaller studios built their own buildings, complete with large screening rooms. Although the buildings are still there, the film industry has left "Film Row."

Of the 100 theaters in Kansas City in 1910, two-thirds were in residential neighborhoods. There were strict ordinances as to where these theaters could be built. By the 1930s the number of theaters had increased and even though the Depression had restricted money for amusements, many felt they could afford 10 cents for a neighborhood double feature — and besides, these theaters offered "Bank Night," giving away money, groceries or dishes. It was entertainment that most could afford once a week.

These neighborhood theaters had names like Bagdad, Gladstone, Isis, Madrid, Colonial, Southtown and Vista. Although some of these buildings remain today, only the Plaza Theater is used for films and it has been remodeled into four smaller theaters. Some of the theater buildings that are still around are unrecognizable. They serve as churches, thrift stores, beauty schools, and warehouses. Many of the early theaters and some of those built later have been torn down or destroyed by fire.

A spectacular fire destroyed the Brookside Theatre in 1978. Built in 1937, it was a popular neighborhood film house. Its design was Colonial which did not quite mesh with the southwest-style interior. A Taos, New Mexico painter, Lloyd Moylan, was hired to paint two 50-foot murals of wagon trains crossing the Santa Fe Trail on the theater's walls. In the foyer he painted scenes of American Indian life. After the fire destroyed the theater, Milgram's grocery store expanded into the space.

Today's moviegoers are used to seeing films in small theaters not at all like the theaters built in the first half of the 20th century. The only grand movie palace left is the Loew's Midland at 1228 Main Street, which presents touring plays, musicals and other special performances.

Members of the "Tower A-Dorables," the dancers at the TOWER THEATER. Jeanne Simpson, Mary Jane Parker and Mary Graham Minor, demonstrate a skating routine on the roof of the theater.
Mary M. Laird

BROOKSIDE THEATRE was a neighborhood movie house located on the east side of Brookside Plaza between 63rd Street and Meyer Boulevard. A fire destroyed the Brookside in 1974.
Kansas City, Missouri Public Library - Missouri Valley Special Collections

MUEHLEBACH FIELD, 22nd Street and Euclid Avenue. Community gardens occupy the site today.
Kansas City, Missouri Public Library - Missouri Valley Special Collections

MUEHLEBACH FIELD

*E*ighty-four years after Abner Doubleday laid out a diamond-shaped playing field for a game he called baseball, the cry of "play ball" resounded at opening day for Muehlebach Field.

George Edward Muehlebach was born in 1881 in the family home at 1736 Main Street, the son of a local brewery owner. While he was a student at Webster School, 1644 Wyandotte Street, he played first base for the Muehlebach Pilsners, a hard-slugging boys baseball team. (In later years he denied that this had anything to do with his adult love of the game.)

Muehlebach went to work in the family business at age 17. Just six years later his father died, and he took over management of the family interests. Young Muehlebach was a baseball fan, regularly sitting in the grandstand at Association Park, 20th and Olive streets, yelling at the top of his lungs for the Kansas City Blues. His friend, team owner George Tebeau, convinced him to buy a small amount of stock in the team in 1915. Within two years he held controlling interest.

He immediately began making plans to improve the team and promised the fans he would build a new home for their Blues. On July 3, 1923, Muehlebach Field officially opened on what had been part of the estate of Dr. Isaac M. Ridge, an early local physician. The single-deck steel and concrete grandstand ran along Euclid Avenue and 22nd Street. Unlike other American Association fields, advertising on the outfield fence — something Muehlebach considered an eyesore — was banned. The owner was willing to take the revenue loss for the beauty of the park.

Muehlebach paced the top of the grandstand through most of that first game. Although opening day was exciting, what he really wanted was a victory. His wish was granted; the Blues beat the Milwaukee Brewers, 10-7. They went on to win the league championship that year and again in 1929, but attendance declined, even after lights were installed in 1931 for night games.

The team changed hands and the ballpark changed names several times. Eventually the park became known as Municipal Stadium and was home to the Kansas City Athletics and later the present Kansas City Royals. After the Royals moved, in 1973, to the Truman Sports Complex, the old ballpark was demolished.

WILLIAM MULKEY residence, 13th and Summit streets. Built 1856; demolished 1907. Nothing remains of the house including the land.
Kansas City, Missouri Parks and Recreation Department

MULKEY HOMESTEAD

A ndrew Drips, a legendary mountain man and Indian trader, built a log cabin on the hills above the West Bottoms in 1838. The land would pass to his son-in-law, William Mulkey, and some of the land would become Kansas City's first park.

Drips and his wife, Macumplamee, an Indian princess, had a daughter, Catherine, who was sent to a St. Louis convent to be educated. She returned home when she was 16. One day, while getting water at the spring on her father's property, Mulkey saw her. He said it was love at first sight; they were married in 1853 by Father Bernard Donnelly.

Mulkey's family, one of the earliest to come to the area, arrived in 1824 from North Carolina when William was four. They settled on the bluffs over-looking the Kaw River, and for a time in 1832, William attended a school run by Mormon leader, Joseph Smith. But the young man did not take to the Mormon religion. Soon Smith and his followers were run out of Jackson County.

Like his future father-in-law, Mulkey became an Indian trader. As the native Americans were pushed off their tribal lands by white settlers, thousands of the Indians came through the town of Westport and the new levee community. The federal govern-ment paid them in silver, so the Indians meant big business for merchants and traders. The Indians reportedly liked and trusted Mulkey because his wife was half Indian and because he always treated them with trust and dignity.

By 1856 Mulkey was ready to build what he called his Western Palace at 13th and Summit streets. It took two years to complete because the bricks were sent from St. Louis at $12 a thousand, and he paid $9,000 in gold (a fortune in those days) for white pine shipped by steamboat from Pittsburgh, Pennsylvania, for the interior walls. Red walnut was brought from California by the way of the Santa Fe Trail for the windowsills, and for the interior beams he cut walnut trees from the dense forest that surrounded the property.

The Classic Revival (Missouri style) mansion had eight rooms, each with a fireplace, and a wide hall on the lower floor. A veranda on three sides of the house offered vistas of both the Missouri and Kaw Rivers.

The Mulkeys, noted for their hospitality, entertained frequently. Mulkey's friend, the famous scout Kit Carson, stayed with the family when he was in the area. Indians were welcome to camp on the property; sometimes as many as 100 tepees could be seen in the Mulkey orchard.

In 1882 William and Catherine Mulkey gave Kansas City a small triangle of land at 16th Street and Belleview Avenue in memory of Andrew Drips. This was the city's first park. By the turn of the century the city wanted to turn a large portion of the West Bluffs, including Mulkey's homestead, into a park that would have tennis courts and baseball diamonds. Mulkey fought the condemnation but eventually took $91,000 for the property.

He wanted his Western Palace preserved as a museum, but the city said the structure was unstable. However, it took dynamite to bring down the brick walls.

Catherine died in 1904 and William in 1907. The little triangle of land they donated in 1882 is all that is left of their land. An inscription on a stone marker has worn with time and is difficult to read. The land at 13th and Summit streets, where Mulkey built his mansion, was excavated to create the Southwest Freeway and Interstate 670.

GEORGE H. NETTLETON HOME FOR AGED WOMEN, 626 Pennsylvania Avenue,
was the first in the city to provide shelter for homeless women.
Kansas City, Missouri Public Library - Missouri Valley Special Collections

GEORGE H. NETTLETON HOME

*H*omelessness is not a new phenomenon. A century ago the plight of an elderly homeless woman led to the founding of the George H. Nettleton Home for Aged Women.

One day in December of 1890, a policeman found a woman wandering along Independence Avenue. He remembered that the Women's Christian Temperance Union had just opened a home for girls at Independence and Lowell Boulevard. Not knowing what else to do, he took the woman there, explained her plight and left. After taking her in, the home began admitting elderly women, and on August 3, 1894, it was renamed the Protestant Home for Aged Women and Girls.

The home moved in 1891 to larger quarters at 29th and Cherry streets. Then, on March 3, 1900, Mrs. George H. Nettleton offered her large Quality Hill home on the northwest corner of Seventh Street and Pennsylvania Avenue, as a permanent residence for elderly women. There was one condition: the name must be changed to the George H. Nettleton Home for Aged Women, in tribute to her late husband.

Nettleton, a self-made millionaire, died in March of 1896. He was the president of the Kansas City, Fort Scott & Memphis Railroad Company. Early in his career he had been responsible for construction of the bridge over the Mississippi River at Quincy, Illinois, and helped to bring the Hannibal & St. Joseph Railroad into Kansas City.

Nettleton's 12-room, gray brick home had been the scene of much entertaining in its day. It was on an acre of ground, commanding a fine view of both the Missouri and Kaw Rivers. George E. Kessler, who designed and supervised the city's highly acclaimed parks and boulevard system, landscaped the grounds around the house.

For over 17 years the facility remained on Quality Hill. But as the Hill declined and the need for space increased, they accepted a tract of land on the east side of Swope Parkway between 51st and 52nd streets, a gift from E. P. Swinney, president of the First National Bank.

The handsome building on Swope Parkway, designed by the local architectural firm of Wilder & Wight, is still a home for elderly women. The house at Seventh Street and Pennsylvania Avenue was demolished.

*NINTH STREET INCLINE was
constructed to bring people to and
from the West Bottoms. The trestle was
demolished in 1905.*
Kansas City, Missouri Public Library -
Missouri Valley Special Collections

NINTH STREET INCLINE

Getting to the West Bottoms was once a challenge. Before the Ninth Street Incline was built in 1885, one way was to follow the banks of the Missouri River west, then circle south on the Kaw River banks west. When the rivers flooded, this route was closed off. There had long been a foot trail from the top of Quality Hill down into the Bottoms. But in bad weather this could be a precarious downhill slide.

Some would say that the Ninth Street cable car was equally dangerous. The cars came down a sharply angled elevated trestle nonstop from the Quality Hill bluffs to the Bottoms. There were two runaway cars on the first day of operations, but no one was seriously injured.

Actually, the Ninth Street car started out on Eighth Street at Woodland Avenue. It swung south on Grand Avenue, around what was called Dead Man's Curve because passengers would be thrown from their seats or the running board when the car was going too fast. The car turned west on Ninth Street, then plunged down the hill, gathering speed toward the Junction at Main Street. Because the brakes were unpredictable, the cars sometimes went right through the intersection. The city's first traffic patrolman was hired to stand at that intersection. He would watch for cable cars and rush out onto the tracks yelling "Wide awake" to alert pedestrians that they should clear the intersection.

From the Junction, the Ninth Street car proceeded uphill until it reached the crest of the Quality Hill bluffs, then it began its descent on the almost perpendicular trestle into the West Bottoms.

The incline was called an engineering marvel of its day. Once at the bottom of the bluffs, cable cars arrived at a wooden station and passengers walked down an enclosed passageway known as "The Cattle Chute" to the street below.

People who lived in Kansas City and worked in the West Bottoms had to face this ride every day — a scary prospect in good weather and even more frightening when there was snow and ice. That may have been why many newcomers to the city who found work in the Bottoms chose to live there as well.

*William Rockhill Nelson's home, OAK HALL, shown before 1900, was the scene of
extensive social activity before its demolition in 1926.*
Landmarks Commission of Kansas City, Missouri

OAK HALL

A t the age of 39, William Rockhill Nelson cast his lot with Kansas City over settling in either St. Louis or Brooklyn, New York. He never regretted his decision, and from his arrival in 1880 until his death in 1915, his presence as a highly respected newspaper editor and civic leader was forever woven into the fabric of Kansas City.

On September 18, 1881, in the first issue of *The Kansas City Evening Star,* (which Nelson and Samuel E. Morss bought shortly after Nelson arrived in the city), the community was alerted to the publisher's agenda: "*The Evening Star* will labor with special zeal and earnestness in behalf of all measures tending to advance the interests of Kansas City and develop the resources of the great Missouri Valley."

Nelson's entire life was that of a builder, and a personal building triumph was his home, Oak Hall. It was built on more than 20 acres of land between what is now 45th Street to Brush Creek Boulevard and Oak Street to Rockhill Road. The original part of the house was constructed in 1887 when the site was about two miles south of the city limits. Most records credit Nelson as having designed it, as well as the additions and changes. Local architects Frederick E. Hill and Louis S. Curtiss are mentioned having served as consultants.

The Romanesque style house was built primarily of locally quarried limestone. Nelson believed in enlarging the house only when dictated by need: by the time "need" was served, the final product was by all standards a mansion. Guests at frequent dinners and receptions could enjoy, among other amenities, the Jacobean oak paneling in the living room. It had been brought as a complete room from Bampfyde House in Exeter, England. When Oak Hall was being demolished, the room was dismantled and later installed in the Nelson-Atkins Museum of Art (built on the site of Oak Hall), where it remained on display until 1989.

Nelson left the house to his wife, Ida, for her lifetime. At her death, six years after her husband's, the house passed to their daughter, Laura Nelson Kirkwood. She died in 1926 at the age of 43. It was stipulated in Nelson's will that Oak Hall be razed and the property be used as a site for an art museum.

Demolition began early in 1928, much to the interest of local residents. Paintings, furnishings and other items from the house that had not been designated for the museum were put on sale to the public. Many residents bought pieces of the house to be incorporated in other buildings. John J. Wolcott bought roof tiles, window frames, stones from the walls,

interior oak paneling and the great oak front door, which were used in the house he was building at 5701 Oakwood Road. The leaded glass bookcases were installed in the library at the Pembroke School for Boys at 7444 State Line Road.

The great room in OAK HALL, with its huge fireplace, oak beams and paneling, was the gathering place for the family.
Kansas City, Missouri Public Library - Missouri Valley Special Collections

THE NINTH STREET THEATER at Ninth and May streets. Built 1886; destroyed by fire 1891; rebuilt as the Orpheum Theater in 1892. This theater was razed in 1922. The land is now used as a surface parking lot.
Kansas City, Missouri Public Library - Missouri Valley Special Collections

Before there was vaudeville there was "variety." This form of entertainment played at the Free and Easy Theater and the Theatre Comique, both on Fourth Street between Main and Delaware streets. There were sketches, impersonations, songs, dances, acrobatic performances and monologues, and the dialogue and situations were often vulgar. Vendors hawked wine, beer and cigars in the audience — these variety houses were supported wholly by men, although occasionally a woman who did not care about her reputation attended.

Abraham Judah built the Ninth Street Theater at Ninth and May streets using money he had made from the Dime Museum. After the theater was destroyed by fire in 1891, H. D Clark, who had owned the Theatre Comique, rebuilt it a year later. Martin Lehman, who had been the manager of the Orpheum Theater in Los Angeles, leased the theater to bring the more family-oriented vaudeville to Kansas City.

In 1898 the theater's name was changed to Orpheum. Although he booked the best acts available, Lehman lost $11,000 the first season because the "variety" stigma was still attached to the presentations. Dividing the city's residential districts into sections, Lehman went from house to house introducing himself, telling people about the kind of entertainment he had to offer and giving away free tickets. He eventually covered the whole town and got people into the habit of going to the Orpheum. Packed audiences saw the country's top vaudeville acts and enjoyed the theater's orchestra, which was made up of the best musicians in town.

The ORPHEUM THEATER'S program for the week of January 28, 1906.
Kansas City, Missouri Public Library - Missouri Valley Special Collections

The theater was such a success that Lehman wanted to move it closer to the Baltimore Hotel and the Willis Wood Theater nearer the heart of downtown.

He built his new 2,300-seat Orpheum at 1212 Baltimore Avenue for $350,000 in 1914. It had a 100-foot frontage and was as tall as a five-story building. It was modern French Renaissance in design; the terra cotta front resembled marble and was decorated with large panels representing music and dance. It took six weeks to lay the marble mosaic floor in the lobby; a mural above the proscenium arch, "Dance of Youth," took four months to paint. An early air-conditioning system operated in the basement of the theater.

The Orpheum was on the Radio-Keith-Orpheum vaudeville circuit, and all of the big stars performed there: Eddie Cantor, Will Rogers, Ed Wynn and Al Jolson, who took home $70,000 for two weeks at the Orpheum.

After World War I, the popularity of vaudeville declined and RKO started producing movies to be played along with vaudeville. By the 1930s the Orpheum was primarily a movie house, showing RKO films featuring such stars as the Marx Brothers and Fred Astaire and Ginger Rogers. Occasionally, however, it would revert to touring stage productions. In the 1950s there were several seasons of plays and musicals featuring leading Broadway stars.

In 1961 the Orpheum was razed to make way for a ballroom addition to the Muehlebach Hotel.

OWL DRUG STORE in the Warder Grand Theater at Ninth and Holmes streets looked like a stage setting.
Kansas City, Missouri Public Library - Missouri Valley Special Collections

KATZ DRUG COMPANY took over the former Owl Drug Store on the northeast corner of Eighth Street and Grand Avenue. The Central Business College was located upstairs.
Kansas City, Missouri Public Library - Missouri Valley Special Collections

OWL AND KATZ DRUG STORES

*T*he drug stores at the turn of the century were more than a place to shop — they were an experience. These old stores had wide aisles and floor to ceiling cabinets that held patent medicines, prescription drugs, soaps, cigars, cigarettes, pipes and tobacco, candies, women's face creams and men's shaving products. At long marble soda fountains, "soda jerks" would dispense banana splits, malts, lemonades and flavored phosphates.

The Owl Drug Store in the Warder Grand Theater building at Ninth and Holmes streets showed just how grand a simple drug store could be. James and Thomas O'Reilly owned a hardware store in Independence but thought a drug store would have higher sales. So in 1888, with an investment of $1,000, they opened their first Owl Drug store in the theater. It was part of a chain based in San Francisco, California.

The O'Reillys advertised extensively and attracted buyers with "cut rate" prices. They opened four stores downtown including one at Eighth Street and Grand Avenue. Later, in 1926 they sold their interest back to the parent company.

The Katz Drug Store with its smiling black cat trade mark was part of the Kansas City scene for 54 years. Their store at Eighth Street and Grand Avenue (formerly an Owl Drug Store), was one of the 40 the company owned in five midwestern cities.

Company founders Isaac and Michael Katz arrived from Poland as children in the 1880s, and with their family settled in St. Paul, Minnesota. Isaac quit school at 13 to travel the rails as a "news butcher." He said later in life that he got his training in merchandising by selling everything from blankets to straw mattresses to men on their way to the gold fields in Alaska during the great Klondike Gold Rush.

In his 20s and newly married, Isaac moved to Kansas City and continued to ride trains out of the Union Depot in the West Bottoms, selling his merchandise. He and his brother opened a store near the depot, selling candy, postcards and souvenirs and within a few years had made $50,000. When the depot closed in 1914 they made their move uptown, opening a confectionery store across from the Empress Theater at 12th and McGee streets.

Wartime restrictions pushed the Katz stores on their way to becoming a success. In 1917 during the First World War a one cent tax was put on cigarettes. The next day's newspaper ad said," "Katz pays the tax" and the slogan caught the public's fancy. Soon the government ordered all stores except drugstores must close at night. The Katz at 12th and McGee streets store made its profits from the night-time theater-going crowd so Isaac hired a druggist and purchased a small supply of drugs so that store could remain open. He made friends with doctors in the nearby Argyle Building and found that filling prescriptions was profitable.

Katz's newspaper ads heralding reduced prices soon had customers flocking to their store. The brothers bought the Owl Drug Stores at Eighth Street and Grand Avenue, at a major streetcar transfer point, as well as other locations. The stores were so successful that by 1925 annual sales were five million dollars.

The brothers' success attracted unwanted attention in 1930. Michael Katz was kidnapped while driving down Ward Parkway and held for $100,000 ransom. The money was paid and Michael was released in the northeast section of town. Three suspects were arrested, but there was not enough evidence to convict them and they were released. After that Michael Katz always rode in a bullet-proof, chauffeur-driven car.

The Katz brothers were civic-minded. They invited the whole city to parties they gave at the Convention Hall (and later, Municipal Auditorium), where free entertainment was provided by top vaudeville and radio performers with appearances of big name movie stars and famous bands. Later the Katz Drug Stores presented an annual free Philharmonic Orchestra (precursor to today's Kansas City Symphony), concert for the public.

Isaac Katz died in 1956, and when Michael died in 1969 it was noted that the company did $53 million worth of business annually. In 1970, the Skaggs Drug Company bought the stores and in 1984 they were taken over by Osco Drugs. The Eighth Street and Grand Avenue store was torn down and today is the site of a surface parking lot.

SUNKEN GARDEN AT 12th Street and THE PASEO. The New York Apartments Building at the right, built in 1903, was demolished as part of the urban renewal policies of the 1970s.
Kansas City, Missouri Parks and Recreation Department

THE PASEO SUNKEN GARDENS

A t the turn of the century The Paseo from Admiral Boulevard south to 17th Street was Kansas City's showplace. Its scenes appeared on more postcards than any other site in the city and the street became famous as the cards were sent around the world.

August R. Meyer, the first president of the Kansas City Park Board, had visited Mexico City and admired the Paseo de la Reforma there. It ran from the capital to the old castle of Chapultepec, where the rulers of Mexico had lived before the Spanish conquest. He wanted to duplicate its cultivated flower beds, trees, ornamental circles, fountains and statues in Kansas City, and he wanted to name it The Paseo.

The first section of the boulevard was finished in 1889. It was a tree-lined road with blocks of parks between its northbound and southbound lanes, landscaped with lavish gardens that included benches, fountains and pools.

There was a large circular fountain in a pool at 15th Street and a beautiful pergola was built at 10th Street. Parallel colonnades supported the pergola's cross beams on which vines grew that filtered the sunlight, providing a sheltered walk. Young girls and their admirers would stroll The Paseo on Sundays under the watchful eye of the girls' mothers. The pergola is still standing and south of 10th and The Paseo is a memorial to Meyer.

The sunken garden from 12th to 13th streets was an inviting place to rest and enjoy the greenery. In the 1970s, though, The Paseo was realigned and much of the garden space was eliminated. Urban renewal has taken most of the grand old buildings that lined the boulevard. By 1990, only one house (built in 1899) remains at 1016 The Paseo.

PENN SCHOOL, 4237 Pennsylvania Avenue was demolished in 1967 following a fire of suspicious origin. Today a surface parking lot occupies the site.
Photograph by Beltron L. Orme

PENN SCHOOL

Charlie "Bird" Parker, (1920-1955) was born in Kansas City and was a graduate of PENN SCHOOL. He was regarded as a jazz, blues and bebop genuis on the alto saxophone.
Kansas City Museum - Kansas City, Missouri

*T*he date Penn School began may well be lost in history. There is reference to a school in that vicinity in 1836 and in 1850. Whatever the date, we know there was some schooling for black children in the Westport area before the Civil War.

The small, vernacular style brick and frame schoolhouse stood in seclusion on a hill in Westport. Following the war, it became apparent that formal education would be needed for the 40 black children in the Westport area, many of them children of freed slaves. The Westport School District acquired the building at 4237 Pennsylvania Avenue in 1869. Penn School, named for William Penn, remained part of the district until 1899, when the district was annexed by the Kansas City Public School District.

The black community Penn School served, just west of St. Luke's Hospital, was centered around two churches: St. Luke's A.M.E. Church at 4260 Roanoke Road (built in 1863, it is the oldest church standing today in Westport) and the more recently constructed St. James Baptist Church at the northwest corner of 43rd and Washington streets, demolished in 1987 after a fire.

As the Country Club area and other wealthy residential sections developed farther south, many of the parents of Penn School pupils found work as maids, cooks and housemen. While at work they observed the customs of the white families and brought them home. Tea parties were held on Sunday afternoon where the social graces were practiced. Many of the black students took music lessons and informal recitals were given.

Mrs. Lillian Orme, Penn School principal from 1953-55, recalled that the children attended the Kansas City Philharmonic concerts. "It was not necessary to tell them how to dress or how to act. They came with their white gloves, in their starched shirts and Sunday shoes."

For most of the school's existence kindergarten through seventh grades were taught, grades four through seven in one room, the younger children in another. Enrollment usually averaged between 60 and 70. Exercises were held outside, weather permitting, as there was no gymnasium.

The families of the pupils held learning in high esteem and good communications between parents, children and faculty kept problems to a minimum. Older students helped younger ones. Graduates went to Lincoln, Central or Manual High Schools. Many have had successful careers as lawyers, doctors, teachers, ministers and scientists. Famous jazz musician Charlie "Bird" Parker graduated from the school.

The United States Supreme Court order to end school segregation and a dwindling enrollment caused the school's closing in 1955. Many people pleaded with the Board of Education to keep it open, arguing that the community would break down without it. Several groups tried to raise money to preserve the building or find a new use for it, but they were unsuccessful.

PLA-MOR, 3142 Main Street, celebrated its grand opening on November 4, 1927. It was built by the Fogel Construction Company. Demolished in 1972, a car dealership occupies the site.
Kansas City Museum - Kansas City, Missouri

PLA-MOR

F our acres of amusements and recreation under one roof — that was what the Pla-Mor offered when it opened in 1927, the largest indoor amusement center in the country at the time. Paul M. Fogel, later to be president of Pla-Mor Amusement Inc., had owned an unsuccessful market in the 3200 block of Main Street. When it closed, he hired Charles A. Smith, the designer of Kansas City's Public school buildings to draw up plans for the recreation complex.

It cost more than $500,000 to build a huge ballroom over the market building, which was converted to house the bowling and billiard facilities. And what a ballroom it was! Five hundred couples glided over the floor on opening night to the music of the Jean Goldkette Orchestra. The dancers likened it to dancing on a cloud — just as they should, since the floor was laid on more than 7,000 hair felt spring cushions with a "give" of a quarter-inch. The crowd of more than 4,000 that night — November 24, 1927 — was so large that five patrolmen were needed to control traffic.

Some of the greatest names in popular music appeared on the Pla-Mor marquee: Glen Gray and his Casa Loma Orchestra, Jimmy Dorsey, Vincent Lopez, Larry Clinton, Stan Kenton and Ella Fitzgerald.

Directly behind the ballroom was the building where the Kansas City Greyhounds ice hockey team played, and where pleasure skaters twirled around an ice rink. The touring Ice Capades show played there every year. In early 1931, excavating began under the ice rink for the construction of the largest fresh-water swimming pool west of the Mississippi River.

With the call to the suburbs growing stronger, midtown began to change. The ballroom closed in 1951, and attempts to keep some entertainment going failed. The building with its familiar marquee is now just a part of Kansas City's entertainment history.

PLA-MOR BALLROOM, was famous for the appearances of some of the giants in the field of popular music.
Kansas City Museum, Kansas City, Missouri

*TEA HOUSE BY THE SIDE OF THE
ROAD was located in a mansion
designed around 1900 by Adriance
and John Van Brunt. It was located at
9 East 45th Street. The Hilton Plaza
Inn was built on the site.*
Herb Simon

*The WISH BONE RESTAURANT was in
a mansion at 4455 Main also built
around 1900. It was razed to make
way for the Plaza Marriott Hotel but
the name "Wish-Bone" lives on as the
name of a well-known salad dressing.*
Wilborn & Associates

RESTAURANTS

*T*wo restaurants stood on 45th Street across from each other, housed in elegant mansions built at the turn of the century. The Tea House by the Side of the Road was on the south side, just east of Main Street. The Wish Bone Restaurant was on the north side. Both opened for business in the 1940s.

Mrs. Harriet Bailey and her sister, Miss Elizabeth Thacher, managed the dining facilities at the downtown Wolferman's store for several years. Their first venture on their own was the original Tea House by the Side of the Road, in the old Hunt Club at 83rd Street and Mission Road.

In 1942 the sisters opened their second tea house just north of the Country Club Plaza at 9 East 45th Street in a mansion designed by the noted Kansas City architects Adriance and John Van Brunt. The Colonial style house, on more than an acre of heavily wooded land, was built sometime around the turn of the century and had been purchased by John Soden in 1921.

The sisters bought it from the Soden estate, converted it into a restaurant and served meals in a genteel manner amidst Victorian furnishings. Diners were served not only in the home's dining room but in the former living room, and library. A stately grand staircase led up from the first floor entrance hallway, and Oriental rugs were in evidence throughout.

The Tea House was razed in 1952; the Hilton Plaza Inn now stands on the site.

The Wish Bone was a family-style restaurant whose main attraction was fried chicken and the special dressing that was served on salads. Joe and Dora Adelman opened the restaurant in 1947 in the former home of Mr. and Mrs. William Chapman. Chapman, a prominent lumberman, with his wife traveled extensively in Europe, the Mediterranean and Asia. They purchased many furnishings and ornaments in their travels. Some they used to decorate their house, others they gave to the Nelson-Atkins Museum of Art. After the Adelmans purchased the house for their restaurant, some of the items the Chapmans had included in the sale decorated the dining and cocktail areas.

The Wish-Bone salad dressing was so popular that many customers asked to take home a sample. The restaurant began to bottle it, selling it in grocery stores throughout the city and soon, nationwide. The restaurant closed in the 1970s. The Marriott Plaza Hotel now stands on the site. The salad dressing can still be found on grocery shelves.

ROTHSCHILD'S on the southwest corner of 10th and Main streets. The building was razed in 1982. Today the land is used as a surface parking lot.
Wilborn & Associates

ROTHSCHILD'S

P hillip Rothschild came to the Town of Kansas in 1853 directly from Germany. He opened a small Indian trading store on the levee. The fort at Leavenworth, Kansas, was gaining in importance, and traffic to that town attracted Rothschild to move there and open a store selling men's hats and women's coats.

The store catered to soldiers and officers and their families at the fort. Among Rothschild's customers were William Tecumseh Sherman and Phillip Sheridan who would become important generals in the Civil War.

Phillip's son, Louis, was brought into the business in 1883. When his father died in 1901, Louis moved the business to Kansas City and opened a store on the southwest corner of 10th and Main streets. The store would remain at this location until the 1980s.

Initially Rothschild's carried only men's furnishings. It was located in Kansas City's financial area, across from the First National Bank and close to many stock brokerage offices. Rothschild's prospered. Architect Frederick McIlvain in 1920-1925 designed a larger store. The builder was the

Fogel Construction. In 1923 Rothschild's expanded to a five-story building south of their location. There was yet another expansion in 1947.

Louis Rothschild, active in community affairs, was one of the founders of Menorah Hospital. He established several Rothschild stores in other parts of the city. But by the 1980s they were closed. The downtown store building was razed to make way for progress...a surface parking lot.

Louis Rothschild, owner of the clothing stores, was one of the founders of Menorah Hospital. This sketch is from As We See Them, *a book by artist "Artigue."*
Kansas City, Missouri Public Library - Missouri Valley Special Collections

SANTA FE CHRISTIAN CHURCH, was located on the north side of Santa Fe Trail. The cemetery remains as does a small portion of the foundation of this unadorned house of worship.   New Santa Fe Historical Society

SANTA FE CHRISTIAN CHURCH

*T*he area, later to be known as Little Santa Fe, was not much more than an Indian settlement in 1824 when the first wagon train passed through. It was on the direct route of the Santa Fe Trail from Independence along the Blue Valley toward Kansas and the Southwest. A log tavern was built there in 1824, followed by a blacksmith shop and a general store.

Early inhabitants on the border between Kansas and Missouri struggled for survival, contending with sporadic border skirmishes and, later, the after-effects of the Civil War. Most of them had to travel 20 miles to Independence for supplies.

Many of the residents, since they had no church of their own, were members of the Bethlehem Church of Christ at Hickman Mills, Missouri. This church, organized by John R. and Elizabeth Whitsett in 1845, had 13 members. They remained as a congregation until about 1869, when the Little Santa Fe contingent organized the Christian church at what is now about 122nd Street and State Line Road. However, no church structure was built until about 1885.

The white frame building that eventually was erected was simple in design, displaying Gothic elements. Worshipers entered through two doors, one for women, the other for men, as was the practice at the time. The little church survived for many years until the J. C. Nichols Company announced plans to extend the Verona Hills subdivision. Efforts by the neighborhood to prevent its demolition came too late. By the time a Jackson County Circuit Court judge had issued a temporary restraining order, it was gone. All that remained on Valentine's Day, 1971, was a bit of rubble.

SCARRITT BIBLE TRAINING SCHOOL AND HOSPITAL at Norledge and Askew avenues in the city's northeast area. It was built in 1892.
Kansas City, Missouri Public Library - Missouri Valley Special Collections

SCARRITT BIBLE TRAINING SCHOOL AND HOSPITAL

*T*he Scarritt Bible Training School, a teaching hospital built to prepare women to become missionaries, was founded in 1892 with a bequest from the Reverend Nathan Scarritt, a pioneer Methodist minister. Scarritt, from Illinois, came to this area in 1851 to teach at the Shawnee Indian Mission in Johnson County, Kansas, and traveled into Indian Territory to preach to the Shawnee, Delaware and Wyandotte Indians. He built a house in the Westport area at what is today 4038 Central Street. (The house is still there). In 1855 he founded and became principal of an early Westport High School.

Antagonism between Kansas and Missouri over the right to own slaves flared into a border conflict before the Civil War. Guerrillas from Kansas made raids on several small communities in Missouri, including Westport. Scarritt decided to move his family north to land he had purchased stretching eastward along the cliffs overlooking the Missouri River. He built a log cabin there; just west of today's Kansas City Museum. When it burned in 1872, he built a 12 room house and platted the land as the Melrose Addition and started what is today the Northeast Neighborhood.

Scarritt became a millionaire from land he had purchased. He had bought 80 acres in Johnson County from the Shawnee Indians and also invested in 20 acres of land in downtown Kansas City from Seventh to Ninth streets, Delaware to McGee streets. He had intended to build a school there but the land became too valuable as the business district pushed southward. He also co-owned the land from 24th to 27th streets, between Main and Oak streets that was platted as the Scarritt-Perry Addition.

Scarritt gave the city the land that became Cliff Drive — or as it is officially known — North Terrace Park. He gave land to each of his 11 children to build homes. Some of these mansions are still there, in back of the Kansas City Museum and on Gladstone Boulevard. He gave the land and money to build the Melrose Methodist Church at 200 North Bales Avenue.

Establishing his missionary training school was his last accomplishment. In the spring of 1890 he traveled to St. Louis to address the Methodist Church Women's Board of Foreign Missions offering to donate the land and $25,000 for the building if the Foreign Missions would match the construction money. He became ill while there, returned to Kansas City and died the next day. The board, not knowing of his death, sent a telegram saying that it would willingly contribute.

The board raised over $100,000 to build the school and create an endowment fund. The facility included a hospital to teach medical techniques to prepare Christian workers for the missionary field. The school also taught courses in church history, sociology, problems of family life, sewing, basketry, kitchen skills, gardening, housekeeping, bookkeeping, music and physical culture.

In 1924 the General Board of Missions of the Methodist Episcopal Church South moved the school to Nashville, Tennessee, and changed its name to Scarritt College for Christian Workers. Later it merged with Vanderbilt University.

In 1931 the school and hospital building in the Northeast were demolished. Houses were built on the site. The surrounding neighborhood is now known as the Scarritt Renaissance Neighborhood.

ST. JOSEPH'S HOSPITAL, located on the northwest corner of Linwood Boulevard and Prospect Avenue, had many features not common then to all local hospitals including refrigerated fever rooms and a telephone in each patient's room.
Kansas City, Missouri Public Library - Missouri Valley Special Collections

ST. JOSEPH'S HOSPITAL.

The old ST. JOSEPH'S HOSPITAL on the west side of Pennsylvania Avenue between Seventh and Eighth streets stood empty and neglected for many years. Before its demolition it bore a sign ironically reading, "Unfit for Human Habitation."
Kansas City, Missouri Public Library - Missouri Valley Special Collections

*I*n 1874, Father Bernard Donnelly invited nuns from the Order of St. Joseph of Carondelet in St. Louis to organize what was to be the city's first private hospital. St. Joseph 's Hospital opened on October 15, 1874 in the 10-room Waterman house at Seventh Street and Pennsylvania Avenue.

The location was thought to be ideal, among the homes of the wealthy Quality Hill families and near the laborers in the West Bottoms. But even though every bed was occupied, the hospital was barely self-sustaining, because many patients were unable to pay. Even so, by 1878 there was a pressing need for additional bed space. The hospital moved to a larger brick building on the property where there was space for 100 patients.

Dr. J. P. Griffith, the hospital's first surgeon, was responsible for much of its success. By today's standards he performed operations with scant and primitive equipment. In 1901 he was instrumental in establishing a nursing school at the hospital.

As the character of Quality Hill changed, the sisters became resigned to searching for yet another site. They purchased property on the northwest corner of Linwood Boulevard and Prospect Avenue with what money they had managed to save and raise by donations. The cornerstone for the new hospital was laid on December 19, 1915, and Bishop Thomas F. Lillis conducted dedication services exactly two years later.

St. Lukes Hospital, Kansas City, Mo.

The Italian Renaissance style building was designed by the distinguished local architectural firm of Wight & Wight. (The Kansas City Life Insurance Company, building [1924], and the Nelson-Atkins Museum of Art, [1930-33] are among other buildings the firm designed.) The fireproof, seven-story hospital was built of red brick in a tapestry over reinforced concrete and steel, in the shape of an X that allowed the greatest amount of sunlight and air into patients' rooms. A sun porch was at the end of each wing.

The hospital was recognized for its modern equipment and methods of treatment. In 1937 the hospital installed the city's first Hubbard Tub to help in the treatment of polio. St. Joseph's Hospital remained a community anchor and source of employment for many years. But, as the population moved southward another move was inevitable. In 1977 the hospital opened at its new location, south of Interstate 435 and just east of State Line Road.

On October 31, 1979, the old hospital was sold to the Linwood Land Corporation for demolition. But the end did not come easily. Only partly demolished because of the lack of funds, it had become fair game for vandals. Mercifully, the building's end came in 1983.

ST. LUKE'S HOSPITAL, another early private hospital, was for 17 years located in this residence on the southeast corner of 11th Street and Euclid Avenue before it was moved to its present Wornall Road location in 1923.
Kansas City, Missouri Public Library - Missouri Valley Special Collections

*The old and the new—ST. PETER AND ST. PAUL CATHOLIC CHURCH (1868)
and the framework of the new Federal Reserve Bank Building (1921) in the
background.*
Kansas City, Missouri Public Library - Missouri Valley Special Collections

ST. PETER AND ST. PAUL CATHOLIC CHURCH

A Catholic priest undoubtedly was the first man of the cloth to visit the Kansas City area, probably in the early 1820s. Those who followed came to open missions for the Indians but failed to stay long. That changed in the 1830s with the Reverend Benedict Roux. From the home of Francois and Berenice Chouteau, Father Roux traveled by horseback throughout the area, visiting Indian tribes. When he purchased land in 1834 to build a church, the Catholics were here to stay. Ten of the 40 acres he bought for six dollars an acre were to be used for a church. There, near the corner of what is now 11th Street and Pennsylvania Avenue, the first permanent Catholic church, a simple log cabin, was built. The Cathedral of the Immaculate Conception now is on the site.

Immigrants of many nationalities, including Germans, were flowing into Kansas City. A few had settled in and around the town before the Civil War, but after the conflict many German Catholics came. A number of them petitioned the diocese for a church where their language would be spoken. In 1868, the Reverend Herman Gross, the priest assigned to the Germans, and a church committee selected a site on the southwest corner of Ninth and McGee streets for a new church. The land was purchased for $2,000.

St. Peter and St. Paul Catholic Church, a handsome red brick Italianate style building, opened in the fall of 1868. Masses were said in both English and German.

In 1870 the much-beloved Father Gross retired due to ill health. The next two years were difficult. Mounting debts led to a discouraged parish, but the arrival of the Reverend Ernest Zechenter brought a turn-around. The parish flourished under his guidance. A school was built in 1882 to accommodate 285 students. Two years later the area between the parsonage and the church was enclosed to become a large hall.

As the city grew many Germans who had lived near the church moved south. Father Zechenter organized another parish for them in 1909, the Guardian Angels Church at 43rd and Mercier streets. The old church struggled on, looking out of place as the grading of Grand Avenue left the building 14 feet above the street level. Undaunted by the new buildings that all but dwarfed the church, the bell that was hung in 1870 continued to mark the hour for masses.

In 1921 the property was leased for development that was inevitable. The church was demolished in 1923. The pipe organ, the first installed in the city, was moved to St. Mary's Hospital chapel; the bell went to Guardian Angels church and the main altar was placed in the Home of the Good Shepherd.

Father Zechenter served as chaplain to St. Mary's Hospital until his death on January 26, 1927.

St. Stephens Baptist Church.
910 HARRISON ST.
KANSAS CITY, MO.

REV. J.W. HURSE D.D.

The Reverend John Wesley Hurse, pastor of ST. STEPHEN BAPTIST CHURCH, led his congregation in a triumphal march to their new church home at 910 Harrison Street. Surface parking now occupies the site.
St. Stephen Baptist Church

ST. STEPHEN BAPTIST CHURCH

*I*f the strength and conviction of one man can be said to inspire and energize a church, John Wesley Hurse was most certainly that man. Hurse was the founder and first pastor of St. Stephen Baptist Church.

Born in 1866 in Tennessee, he had little if any formal education. Hurse left home at the age of 20 and came to Kansas City where he worked at a variety of odd jobs. He found time to attend the Washington School of Correspondence to satisfy his burning desire to read the Bible. It took six years, but he received his doctor of divinity degree.

Hurse ministered to people who lived in areas known as "Bellevidere Hollow," "Hick's Hollow," and "Hell's Half-Acre." These areas were north and west of Independence Avenue, where residents were mostly black or Italian. Converts were baptized in the Missouri River.

St. Stephen Baptist Church was formally organized in 1903 in a tent at Independence Avenue and Charlotte Street. Pastor Hurse and his congregation soon realized the church must find its own building. Their first move was to an existing building at 604 Charlotte Street. But the church burned before a service could be held. It was rebuilt, largely by members of the congregation, and opened in August 1905.

By 1922 the building had become too small. Later that year the congregation bought the Central Presbyterian Church at 910 Harrison Street for $37,000. It was an imposing, Gothic Revival style building with a slate roof and an interior like a "proper church" — carpeting, a pipe organ, rooms for religious use and a real pulpit.

Two spectacular spires — the taller one 120 feet high — made it easy to identify on the horizon. Unfortunately, the congregation could not afford to maintain the spires. The taller one was brought down on August 28, 1923, the other a short time later.

Hurse died on October 14, 1935. Less than three years later, just before dawn on February 15, 1938, fire struck the church. The blaze was well under way by the time the alarm was sounded, and the wooden floors and furniture already were burning. Little remained of the building after the fire was extinguished.

Once again a new building had to be found. Less than a month after the fire, the congregation rented a building at 1414 East 15th Street, the former site of the Paseo Ballroom. In 1941 the congregation, happy with the location, bought the building and eventually the entire block. Over time, remodeling has removed all traces of the ballroom.

ST. TERESA'S ACADEMY (about 1900) located on the west side of Washington Street between 11th and 12th streets. Built 1866; demolished 1916. A parking garage occupies the site today.

Students in a typical ST. TERESA'S ACADEMY boarding room (about 1885).
St. Teresa's Academy

ST. TERESA'S ACADEMY

*L*ed by Sister Francis Joseph Ivory, five nuns from the Order of St. Joseph of Carondelet left St. Louis for Kansas City in 1866 at the request of Father Bernard Donnelly to open a convent. A site on the west side of Washington Street between 11th and 12th streets was chosen. To the west was a small log church built in 1835 by Father Benedict Roux. To the north the settlement of the Town of Kansas and the junction of the Missouri and Kaw Rivers.

The nuns opened a school — first known as St. Joseph's Academy — in 1866, almost two years before the first public school opened in the city. The name was changed to St. Teresa's Academy in 1867.

Laura Coates, daughter of civic leader Colonel Kersey Coates, was the first of 150 boys and girls to register on opening day. The school was popular both as a day school and a boarding school. These were the days of the westward movement. Families frequently were left behind as the father spent long stretches of time on the trails going west or panning for gold. Daughters often were left to the safekeeping of the academy.

Solid academic courses were taught under the direction of Mother Mary Depazzi, the first principal. Also required of the girls were studies in womanly accomplishments common to all the old-time boarding schools, including ornamental needlework, lace-making and tapestry.

The school building, originally designed by architects Francisco, Switzer and Jefferies, was enlarged over the years, but when Quality Hill began to deteriorate, St. Teresa's moved in 1910 to its present site at 56th and Main streets. A statue of St. Joseph, given to the school by Colonel Kersey Coates, made the move to the new location, as did the old chapel bell "that used to sweeten the memories of those who dwelt within its sound, remembering early days."

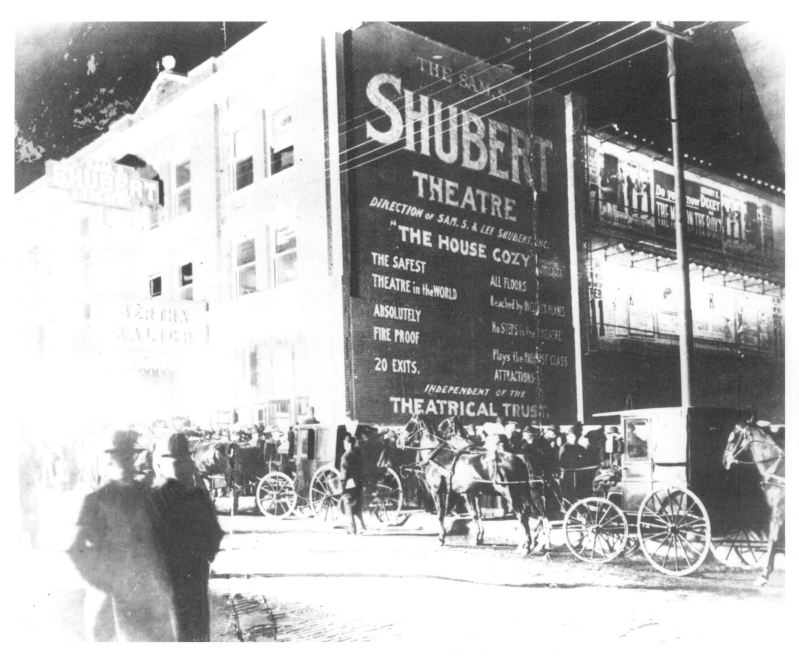

SHUBERT THEATER on the northwest corner of 10th Street and Baltimore Avenue. It was razed in 1935 and the land is now a parking lot for Boatman's First National Bank.
Kansas City, Missouri Public Library - Missouri Valley Special Collections

Compact construction that brought the audience close to the actors on stage gave the Shubert Theater its nickname: "The House Cozy." The Shuberts produced notable plays and musicals in their theater in New York and owned 150 first-class show places in all the major cities in America. They declared the one in Kansas City was their best and dedicated it to Sam S. Shubert, who was killed in a railroad accident in 1905 on his way to Kansas City to negotiate for the theater's construction.

Red was the prevailing interior color — the plush silk curtain and wall hangings were red, as was the carpet that (unlike that in other theaters) covered the entire floor, even under the seats. The stage was 40 by 45 feet, and there were 20 dressing rooms. The lobby floor was done in mosaic, and the name of Sam Shubert was worked into its design.

The Shuberts said they were prepared to spend one million dollars to safeguard the theater from fire, because there had been many theater fires throughout the country in which lives had been

lost. The architect, Charles E. Fox of Marshall & Fox, of Chicago was charged with gathering all information available about fire walls and curtains and was told to provide 20 exits. Builder Leo N. Leslie made all the floors of concrete, even the balcony.

Because the Shuberts owned so many theaters and were an institution on New York's Broadway, they toured only the best shows and performers. But the popularity of silent films drew people away from stage productions and, with the advent of sound, more were attending movie theaters. The Shubert changed hands several times, later belonging to the Orpheum circuit, then O. D. Woodward. Eventually it came back to Shubert management.

Although several outstanding films had their premieres at the Shubert, it remained primarily a stage for live productions, unlike many other theaters. It outlived many of its competitors.

The cover of a SHUBERT THEATER program.
Kansas City, Missouri Public Library - Missouri Valley Special Collections

*From the early 1920s until the 1970s
SIGNBOARD HILL was a prime place
for billboards. Now both the ads and
the hill are gone but some of the
outcropping of rocks is still there on
Main Street under the Westin Crown
Center Hotel.*
Wilborn & Associates.

SIGNBOARD HILL

*M*any visitors to Kansas City are amazed that the area is hilly. They expect a flat terrain, because the city is on the edge of the plains. But land in the city rises from 800 feet above sea level to 1,081 feet at its highest point.

Early visitors to Kansas City found bluffs as high as 100 feet just behind the levee separating the riverfront from the forest beyond. The rain-formed gullies between the hills were used as Indian trails and later would become Main and Market streets (Market Street later became Grand Avenue), the first roads south to Westport. Oxen pulling freight wagons bound for Santa Fe, New Mexico, had a steady climb up the hills from the riverfront to Westport.

The halfway point was OK Creek, about 21st Street. It was difficult to ford, because when it flooded, water ate away at its banks. (The creek still flows underground, in large pipes laid under the railbeds that lead to Union Station). The road to Westport continued south, passing through high bluffs on the creek's banks. Once the wagons reached 31st Street there was a leveling off.

Part of these bluffs south of OK Creek lasted until the 1970s as Signboard Hill. This was a 75-foot-high rocky hill that stood east of the Liberty Memorial from Main Street to Grand Avenue, south of Pershing Road. It received its name May 17, 1923, from A. E. Hutchings, chairman of the Liberty Memorial Site Protection Association, in a speech to the Women's Commercial Club, because the hill had 77 signs on it. The next day an article in *The Kansas City Star* quoted: "In the daylight they (the signs) are vivid with colors; at night, their flashing lights are an irritating reminder that commercialism has elbowed its way to what would appear to be a vantage point to shout its wares."

It was estimated that leveling the more than 10 acres covered by the hill would cost one million dollars and because the earth and rock would occupy 50 percent more space once loosened, getting rid of the debris also was a problem.

Many suggestions for the hill were offered: a post office building (later built across from and west of Union Station), a city hall and courthouse (built downtown in 1936), a 30,000 seat municipal stadium and low-cost housing. In 1946, there was a proposal to build a World War II memorial.

But nothing happened until Hallmark Cards, Inc., developed Crown Center in the early 1970s. The east side of Signboard Hill was leveled for the shops and the Westin Crown Center hotel was constructed on what remained. Although there is evidence of the hill on the west side of the hotel, most of it is gone.

To some, Signboard Hill was an eyesore. To others, though, the colorful signs on the hill were a landmark.

SISTERS OF MERCY HOME FOR GIRLS was opened in 1887 at 510 East Sixth Street.
Sisters of Mercy

ST. AGNES CONVENT was built in 1902 at Hardesty and Scarritt avenues in the northeast section of the city. Today there is a retirement and nursing home on the property.
Sisters of Mercy

SISTERS OF MERCY HOME
FOR GIRLS
ST. AGNES CONVENT

*I*n 1887 Catholic Bishop John J. Hogan was concerned that good homes be provided for the many single women in the city. He sent for two nuns, Mother Agnes Dunn and Sister Mary Edmund Whelan of the order of the Sisters of Mercy from Louisville, Kentucky. They opened the Sisters of Mercy Home, a boarding house for working women at 510 East Sixth Street that attracted not only boarders but young women who wanted to join the order. This was the start of a teaching order that still serves Kansas City.

The boarding house was so successful that the nuns were asked to take over the teaching of St. Patrick's School at Eighth and Cherry streets. The Sisters saw a need for a high school for their students and a convent as more women showed interest in joining the order.

Mother Agnes found land in the northeast section of the city just off St. John Avenue on Hardesty Avenue. She died before her dream became a reality but Sister Mary Edmund purchased the land and by 1902 the first wing of St. Agnes School and Convent opened with two students.

Within a short time there were enough students that an addition was needed. The school had both day and boarding students. One of the early boarding students was Billie Cassin, later known as film actress Joan Crawford.

St. Agnes Convent became the motherhouse of the Sisters of Mercy who were also nurses at St. John's Hospital and taught at St. Peter's School and St. Mary's Academy in Independence (under the name of St. Mary's High School, it is still thriving.) The Sisters of Mercy were the only order with a motherhouse and novitiate in Kansas City until 1929 when the novitiate was transferred to Omaha.

St. Agnes' scholastic reputation grew over the years as did the enrollment and need for expansion. In 1940 the school decided to accept male students and changed its name to Cardinal Glennon High School. Buildings were constructed including a gymnasium and the boy's sports teams won many trophies competing against schools throughout the metropolitan area.

By the late 1960s enrollment had declined. The school closed in 1971 and the property was sold. Buildings were torn down and new buildings were constructed to accommodate a retirement and nursing home. A few of the older nuns still live in a small residence hall built for them in 1964 on the north edge of the campus.

GILLIS HOTEL, was built on the levee in 1849. It was demolished in 1909. Today the land is a holding place for coal for the Kansas City Power and Light Company's downtown steam plant at 115 Grand Avenue.
Kansas City, Missouri Public Library - Missouri Valley Special Collections

TROOST/GILLIS HOUSE HOTEL

*T*here was not much skyline to the town in the 1850s: a few small warehouses on the levee, some log cabins and bluffs that rose 80 to 100 feet behind them. The town was just east of the confluence of the Missouri and Kaw Rivers, near the natural rock ledge that was used as a docking place for boats. The four-story brick Troost House Hotel, facing the river between Delaware and Wyandotte streets, reassured arriving steamboat passengers that there was a town here.

Kansas City's first hotel was built in 1846 by Thompson McDaniel on the southwest corner of Market street and the levee. It offered the barest shelter: just one big open space with a bar, sitting and sleeping room.

In 1849, realizing the discovery of gold in California would bring many through the area, William Gillis and Dr. Benoist Troost built a four-story hotel, naming it after the doctor. It became the stopping-off place not only for those with gold fever, but for the tide of settlers seeking new lands in the West, merchants wanting to sell freight to Santa Fe traders, and pro and anti-slave activists interested in the outcome of Kansas statehood.

The hotel played a role during Missouri-Kansas border conflicts before the Civil War. At different times it was the headquarters of groups both for and against slavery. Those in favor of the South threatened to burn it down, so the owners turned it over to W. H. Chiles a known advocate of slavery and a gambler. He changed the name to the American, and it became known for gambling as well as lodging.

In 1856 the anti-slave group, New England Emigrants Society, took over the hotel and named it the Eldridge, after one of its leaders. During this time pro-slavery border supporters threatened to kill A. H. Reeder, governor of the Kansas Territory. He was hidden in the hotel, then taken to safety disguised as a laborer. In 1858 Colonel N. C. Clairborne bought the hotel and named it after himself. Then in 1861, Gillis and a partner bought it back and named it the Gillis.

During this time New York and other eastern cities had luxury hotels. The Gillis hardly fit that category. The 8-by-10 foot rooms had beds but little other furniture. Then again, it was the only resting place for those who were traveling west. The 60-room hotel's register included names from Europe, South America and Asia: more than 27,000 lodgers signed the register in 1856 when steamboat traffic was at its height. People bunked in the common bar, in a long hall, on parlor floors and on the veranda.

A large bell in the hotel's cupola was rung every morning and announced all meals. A table accommodating 60 diners was set up in the bar, but since the town had no other public eating place, the hotel served meals to many more.

Civic leaders saw the need for more lodging and organized a hotel committee. The Wayside Inn at 16th Street and Grand Avenue, the Union Hotel on the southeast corner of Main Street and Missouri Avenue, and the Pacific House Hotel at Fourth and Delaware streets (the building still stands), were built between 1858 and 1868. When Kersey Coates built the Coates House in 1870, its relative luxury drew clientele away from the older hotels.

The town's expansion southward by the mid-1870s and the shift of westward travelers from steamboats to trains sent the riverfront hotels into decline. By the end of the century the hotel that Troost and Gillis built had a reputation as a brothel. Fires over the years damaged the building, but a portion survived until 1909. Its last occupant was a pickle factory.

VAUGHAN'S JUNCTION

For Kansas City, 1869 was a milestone. That was the year the Hannibal Bridge over the Missouri River opened and Major Samuel D. Vaughan, a real estate dealer, commissioned architect Asa Beebe Cross to design a building of note.

A four-story, Second Empire style building was constructed on land Vaughan had purchased at the junction of Ninth, Delaware and Main streets. The building was remembered for its height and its Mansard roof, an unusual type for a local office building.

In the late 1860s the city's population was slightly over 6,000. Its southern limit was 20th Street and streets had not yet been paved. Most business establishments were along the riverfront. Not daunted by these facts, Vaughan saw promise in his location. A little more than five years proved him right: unfortunately, he was an early victim of the 1873 bank panic. The building was sold in late 1872 at a sheriff's sale for $31,790. Business activities all but came to a halt during the panic, but by the early 1880s a sense of coming prosperity had set in. As evidence, the Kansas City Times Company bought the building, known as the Junction Building, for $85,000 — considered an exorbitant price.

The site had become the busiest corner in the city. It was where the cable carline that connected the east side of town with the West Bottoms slowed down before dashing madly down the Ninth Street Incline into the West Bottoms.

The building proved to be a successful investment. On March 1, 1886, the First National Bank with capital of $250,000 and deposits of $513,000, opened quarters in the first floor tip of the building.

As business began creeping south and east, the prestige of the Junction Building waned. However in 1911, much to the amazement of the business community, the Williams Reality Company bought the building and a companion structure built by the Kansas City Times Company, for $300,000.

By 1916, the old Junction Building had been razed and the 11-story Westgate Hotel, designed by the architectural firm of McKecknie & Trask, had been completed. It was considered a businessmen's hotel, but its main claim to fame may well have been that there, "Shipwreck Kelley" broke the old flagpole-sitting record of 125 hours, 1 minute with a new record of 140 hours, 43 minutes. He said he chose the Westgate's pole because it offered such good visibility. The building, later known as the Hotel Kay, was demolished in 1954.

VAUGHAN'S "DIAMOND", (the JUNCTION BUILDING), was at the time of its construction in 1869 the most pretentious building in town. Today "The Muse of the Missouri" fountain is in the traffic island on the site.
Kansas City, Missouri Public Library - Missouri Valley Special Collections

UNION DEPOT, on Union Avenue just east of Santa Fe Street. Built 1877/78; razed 1915. Today railroad tracks cut across the land where once it stood.
Kansas City, Missouri Public Library - Missouri Valley Special Collections

Eight railway companies shipped Kansas City goods around the country from Union Depot. Houses were built into the cliffs above the tracks and mansions perched at the top of the Quality Hill bluffs.
Kansas City, Missouri Public Library - Missouri Valley Special Collections

UNION DEPOT

When civil leaders saw the design for the Union Depot to be built in the West Bottoms in 1877, many called it "Kansas City's Insane Asylum." This was not only because they thought the railroads would never need such a large building, but also because its builder, James A. McGonigle, was constructing a hospital for the insane in Topeka. (During the eight months it took McGonigle to construct the depot he not only built the hospital, he built Creighton College in Omaha and the Kansas Pacific depot in Topeka.)

The Union Depot was built on land leased from Colonel Kersey Coates. Within two years passengers and freight filled it and an annex larger than the original depot building had to be built. At the time it represented something new in architecture and created a great deal of interest throughout the country. Noted architect Asa Beebe Cross and his pupil and junior partner, William M. Taylor, designed it in the Renaissance style to resemble a French palace.

The architects said it was a parallelogram, 348 feet long and 50 feet wide. The central tower over the main entrance was 125 feet high and had clocks on all four sides. There were dormers, arches, cornices and spacious doorways. Inside were handsome fluted iron columns.

Eight railroads used the depot and since the trains ran on coal and their smokestacks belched black dust, the depot was soon encrusted with grime inside and out. The thousands of passengers who used the depot had to watch their step, as the train tracks ran level with the sidewalk outside the depot and criss-crossed the cobblestones on Union Avenue.

The street was a busy place. The Blossom House Hotel and Eyssell's Drug Store were up the street from the depot. For passengers with time to kill between trains there were small restaurants, a tattoo parlor, beer and gambling halls, brothels and other forms of entertainment.

In 1903 the Missouri River flooded the West Bottoms and filled the Union Depot. It stopped all train traffic. Civic leaders started looking for a place on high ground to build another depot. When the Union Station at Main Street and Pershing Road was completed in 1914, a closing celebration was held for the Union Depot on Halloween Night. There was a band and a large crowd gathered to bid the depot farewell. The last tickets were sold for the final train. As it pulled out of the depot, everyone went out on Union Avenue to watch as the depot's windows and doors were nailed shut. They were not only saying goodbye to the depot but also to the wide variety of activity that had revolved around it.

In 1918 the Mayor's Committee built this VICTORY ARCH north of 11th Street on Grand Avenue for those coming home who had fought in the First World War.
Wilborn & Associates

VICTORY ARCHES

World War I was called The Great War and The War to End All Wars. In the 19 months the United States fought in the war, 5,000,000 Americans volunteered or were drafted to fight Germany. By Armistice Day, November 11, 1918, 440 Kansas City men and one woman, a nurse, had lost their lives in the fighting.

In September 1898, a victory arch had been built at Ninth Street and Grand Avenue to welcome home volunteers from Missouri's 3rd Regiment who had returned from Cuba, where they had fought in the Spanish-American War. Area residents awaiting their loved one's return from World War I donated money to build similar victory arches.

Crowds were willing to come out for parades in the spring of 1919. But they had kept to their homes the previous fall, afraid of the spreading Spanish influenza thought to have been brought to this country by those returning from the battlefields. The flu eventually killed 548,000 in the United States, five times the number of Americans killed in the war.

By October 1918, the flu had killed 425 Kansas Citians and 120 new cases were being reported each day; schools, theaters, churches and other public buildings were ordered closed. Lumberman Robert A. Long offered to underwrite all costs of a proposal to convert Convention Hall into a hospital. An autumn freeze seemed to stop the spread of the disease. By Armistice Day, schools and other places had reopened.

The victory arches were temporary structures built by the Kansas City Scenic Company. Canvas was stretched over wooden frames and then painted to resemble marble. One of the arches was on Grand Avenue between 10th and 11th streets. Another was constructed just east of the Union Station on Pershing Road where it greeted returning servicemen when they left their trains.

The arch near 11th Street was the largest: 90 feet high and 24 feet thick. A painted mural depicted battles and victories, and a sculptured figure of Justice crowned the top of the main archway. Figures of a Red Cross nurse, a soldier, a sailor and a Marine stood atop smaller arches over the sidewalks.

All through the spring of 1919 these returning men and women marched triumphantly through the arches while crowds cheered. It was a happy time. The boys were back. The war was over and there was only peace to look forward to.

A VICTORY ARCH was built at Ninth Street and Grand Avenue in 1898 to welcome home soldiers from the Spanish American War.
Native Sons Collection

Originally the first four floors of the WALDHEIM BUILDING, 6 East Petticoat Lane, were used for retail stores with office space on the floors above.
Kansas City, Missouri Public Library - Missouri Valley Special Collections

WALDHEIM BUILDING

F or well over a half-century the Waldheim Building was part of the two-block corridor that was called Petticoat Lane. It was built for the May Stern Realty Company of St. Louis. The company's president was Louis A. Waldheim.

The Chicago School style office and retail building, completed in 1910, was designed by Daniel H. Burnham & Company of Chicago. The George A. Fuller Company, also of Chicago handled its construction. (They also built Kansas City's Union Station.)

The brick building with terra cotta facing on the west and south sides, was so tall — 16 stories — that it commanded a strong visual presence along Petticoat Lane. Although ornamentation was sparse, Burnham did incorporate a terra cotta cornice on the third story and slightly more elaborate decorations on the 16th floor. Chicago style windows (a fixed central pane flanked by narrow, operable windows) were used on the second and third floors, while the remaining floors had double-hung windows.

Daniel H. Burnham & Company was the successor of the architectural firm of Burnham & Root, which had been widely acclaimed for the marvelous design of the Rookery Building in Chicago. After Root's death in 1891, Burnham designed the Union Station in Washington, D. C. (1907).

The Waldheim Building, demolished in 1986, fell victim to the explosion of downtown development. One Petticoat Lane Building now occupies the site.

*The grounds of THE WALNUTS, the
Tudor-style stone home of W. W.
Sylvester was a showplace, landscaped
with hundreds of shrubs and trees.*
The Kansas City Star Company

THE WALNUTS

*T*he visual presence of the three substantial 10-story apartment buildings near the northeast corner of 51st Street and Wornall Road is testament to the fact that big walnuts from little ones grow.

On the same site in 1905 (then 51st Street and Broadway), W. W. Sylvester had built a handsome Tudor style residence on 10 acres, which he called The Walnuts. It was designed by Adriance Van Brunt, who that same year had designed Shelter House No. 1 at the entrance to Swope Park. When the home was built, the property was outside the city limits. That same year, J. C. Nichols made his first land purchase near 51st and Main streets.

The Walnuts, built of native limestone, boasted one of the city's finest pipe organs in a room off the first-floor landing. It also could accommodate a small orchestra. On the third floor was an oft-used ballroom. The beautiful grounds were much admired by members of the Kansas City Country Club, which was located diagonally across the street.

In 1917, Sylvester sold the property to Wallace N. Robinson, formerly of Tulsa, Oklahoma, who, at about the same time, acquired controlling interest in the Baltimore Hotel. By the late 1920s the character of the area had begun to change. The Country Club Plaza was well under way. High-rise apartments were surrounding the Plaza, making the 10-acre Walnuts site more marketable for multifamily housing. By the end of 1928, the C. O. Jones Company announced plans for the construction of the apartments buildings, designed by architects Boillot & Lauck, who were responsible for the design of the original Unity Village.

The 36 cooperatively owned luxury suites were completed in 1930.

AUDITORIUM THEATER on the northeast corner of Ninth and Holmes streets.
Built 1887; demolished 1945. A surface parking lot is now on the site.
Kansas City, Missouri Public Library - Missouri Valley Special Collection

THE WARDER GRAND/AUDITORIUM THEATER

*T*he opening of the Warder Grand Theater had to be delayed one night so that cast-iron stoves could be installed backstage to keep the actors from freezing. The building was not finished; there was no roof, no heating system and no theater seats. It finally opened the next night, using chairs borrowed from a funeral home.

Edwin Booth, brother of Abraham Lincoln's assassin, John Wilkes Booth, played the leading role of "Othello" on opening night, October 26, 1887. He played to a $50-a-seat audience that was wrapped in furs and blankets. A review in *The Kansas City Times* said: "Mr. Booth succeeded in rousing a good deal of enthusiasm, notwithstanding adverse condi-tions. Beyond a doubt it was the most uniquely marvelous first night on record."

Colonel George Woodward Warder built the theater in the last days of the 1880s real estate boom. Costs, over $350,000, ran higher than expected; by 1890, Warder had lost his fortune and the Bank of Commerce foreclosed on the building. The theater continued to present leading performers of the day until fire destroyed it in 1897.

Another, named the Auditorium Theater, was built in its place. It had a seating capacity of 2,000 and its stage, called the largest in the country, was so mammoth that a team of horses pulling a carriage could complete a circular turn. An elephant was brought on stage for one production and there was still plenty of room for the players.

After the Willis Wood Theater opened on Baltimore Avenue the top performers no longer preferred the Auditorium. The theater put together its own stock company and successfully produced old and new plays at an admission price of 10 cents. Families of limited means became seasoned theatergoers. But by World War I, motion picture theaters were pulling audiences away from live performances, and the theater closed.

For a time the Great Western Stage Equipment Company used the building to construct scenery for locally produced plays. Later, it was used as a warehouse and a hotel. In 1942 the owners an-nounced plans to remodel the building into a movie theater and a 26-room hotel, but they never followed through.

In 1945 a 100-foot section of the theater's north wall collapsed and the building was razed.

IRVING/ BOOKER T. WASHINGTON SCHOOL, 2404 Prospect Avenue, opened in 1886. For over 100 years the building was a familiar part of the Prospect Avenue streetscape.
Landmarks Commission of Kansas City, Missouri.

IRVING/BOOKER T. WASHINGTON SCHOOL

*I*rving School opened in the Town of Kansas in 1886, a year before the city officially became Kansas City.

The original section of the Romanesque Revival style building was designed by William F. Hackney. Additions in 1907 and 1914 were the work of Charles A. Smith who had been Hackney's partner and succeeded him as the architect for the Kansas City, Missouri School Board. The two rounded arches defined the main entrance that faced Prospect Avenue. When the school opened it had 16 rooms but was later expanded. The red brick exterior displayed turrets and gables piercing the roof slope.

The Board of Education changed the school's name in 1945 to Booker T. Washington School, reflecting the growing number of black children in the neighborhood.

An obsolete and antiquated building in the 1970s that demanded more and more investments for repairs, the school was forced to close. Vacant and unattended, the building was a victim of fires and vandalism. Even though the building showed signs of ravages, it was regarded as a landmark and culturally important to the community. Efforts toward adaptive reuse were not successful. Hoping to open a black cultural center, the school board agreed to sell the building to a group if it could raise money for the restoration as well as the purchase price. This failed. Early in 1990 the building was demolished.

WASHINGTON SCHOOL BUILDING, KANSAS CITY, MO.

WASHINGTON SCHOOL, moved into this building in 1867. Located on the
northwest corner of Independence Avenue and Cherry Street, it was the city's first
public school. It was demolished in the 1950s to make way for the Sixth Street
Trafficway.
Kansas City, Missouri Public Library - Missouri Valley Special Collections

WASHINGTON SCHOOL

*T*he Civil War was finally over. Families were beginning to reassemble after being scattered by Order No. 11, (issued in 1863 by General Thomas Ewing, requiring residents of several Missouri counties to move within one mile of a military post. It was intended to discourage guerrilla warfare and the harboring of Confederate soldiers.)

Children and the elderly found the Order to be a hardship in that it disrupted family life and brought education almost to a halt. Only a few private and parochial schools continued to hold classes.

With the end of the war, the larger need for education had to be addressed. Public education began in Kansas City in 1866, when the Kansas City Public School District was organized under state law. The Board of Education was formed the following year and citizens began paying taxes to support free public education.

Washington School was the first to open in 1867. Classes were held in a rented building for one year until the first public school house, on the southwest corner of Independence Avenue and Cherry Street, was finished. The two-story building, designed by Asa Beebe Cross, had a bell tower that appeared to be out of proportion with the rest of the building.

Children from both poor and wealthy families attended. The city limits extended south to 23rd Street by this time although the population center still was concentrated between the Missouri River and Independence Avenue. Wealthy families were living on Quality Hill and Pearl Street, north of Second Street between Walnut Street and Grand Avenue. Poor families, mostly immigrants, lived in tenements around the City Market.

Attendance was not mandatory, as some of the poorer children had jobs. The fortunate ones, those who had clothing and shoes and did not need to work, came for an education.

Washington School was a true melting pot. There were Italians, Swedes, Greeks, Sicilians, a few Russians and some Chinese. Many came to school not speaking a word of English. The language barrier must have been formidable. This did not discourage the Misses Julia M. Stukenburg and Mary Sams who came to the school as young women and taught for more than forty years with patience and affection.

Enrollment dwindled as the residential areas moved south. The school's doors closed in 1926, and it was sold by the school district. After various commercial uses, it was one of the more than one-hundred and twenty buildings swept away for the construction of the Sixth Street Trafficway.

Constructed along the banks of Indian Creek, WATTS MILL served farmers for miles around with custom grinding, which meant the miller kept a certain portion of the grain as his pay for the work.
Kansas City, Missouri Public Library - Missouri Valley Special Collections

The original part of the WATTS HOME was constructed in 1854. A two-story addition was added later.
Kansas City, Missouri Public Library - Missouri Valley Special Collections

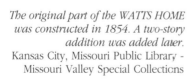

F or those who heeded the call to head west there were fortunes to be made. The lures were furs, gold and silver. Captain William Bicknell led the way. In August 1822, Bicknell, regarded as the founder of the Santa Fe Trail, left what was then known as Franklin, Missouri, with wagons loaded with merchandise. He arrived in Santa Fe, New Mexico, in November of the same year. This first successful trip on the trail opened the floodgates, resulting in a steady stream of wagon trains passing through the Kansas City area on their way west and southwest. In those early days one of the stops on the part of the trail that was to the south of Kansas City was a mill in western Jackson County. It was one of the last "civilized" areas before crossing onto the prairie. The area around the mill would later be called Dallas.

Some early accounts say the grist mill at the bend along the banks of Indian Creek was built in 1832. The mill definitely existed when Anthony B. Watts and his wife Sally, a great-grand daughter of Daniel Boone, settled there in 1850 with their 11 children.

What they found was a small 20-foot square mill building made of hand-hewn walnut and white oak timbers, held together with hickory pins. The burrs for grinding had come from France. Each burr was about four feet in diameter, 14 inches thick, and made of a high-grade sandstone with quartz veins. The grinding surface was grooved with shallow trenches, which required frequent recutting as they wore down quickly. One burr was mounted above the other. Grain was fed through a hole in the running or top stone onto the ground or bottom stone. The ground stone remained stationary; the running stone, powered by water from the creek, turned at about 12 to 15 revolutions per minute, forcing the grain to the edges, where it was caught. The mill had two sets of stones, one for wheat and one for corn. The grain products were graham, whole wheat and buckwheat flour, and exceptionally good cornmeal. The mill was patronized not only by westward-bound travelers but also the area Indians. Business was primarily controlled by the weather. The mill was forced to close in the winter when the creek froze or during the summer, when the creek ran dry.

Watts died in 1861. Stubbins Watts, the ninth of his children, (born in 1838) succeeded his father as the miller. Stubbins, then 23, and his wife Nancy also occupied the Watts home a few hundred feet from the mill. The original part of the two-story house had been built in 1854 and was expanded later. Across the creek from the mill was the farm belonging to Jim Bridger, a famous mountain man, Indian fighter and friend of Watts. (In later years, Stubbins easily recognized by his long, white beard, became known as "The Fiddling Miller of Dallas." Among his favorite tunes were "The Irish Washerwoman" and "Turkey in the Straw.")

Following Stubbins' death in 1922, his three children took over operation of the mill. Because the building had become unsafe it was closed in 1942. As a contribution to America's war effort, Edgar Watts that same year donated nearly nine tons of the mill's iron machinery to the World War II scrap metal drive. The mill was demolished in 1949. The exact date of the demolition of the Watts' house is unknown.

The property is now owned by the Kansas City, Missouri Parks and Recreation Department, which has planned a park around a reconstruction of a working mill and the Jim Bridger farmhouse.

MR. and MRS. STUBBINS WATTS are shown seated behind the Watts home. They, along with several other members of the family, are buried in the Pleasant Valley Cemetery near Stanley, Kansas.
Jackson County Historical Society

WEBB CASTLE was built in 1904 outside of the city's limits. Ruins of the castle can still be seen at 8600 Truman Road - east of Interstate 435.
Jackson County Historical Society

WEBB CASTLE

*T*he shell is all that remains of Webb Castle. Because of its gloomy appearance and its location opposite the Mount Washington Cemetery on Truman Road, the castle was rumored to be haunted, and the legend persisted that those disturbing the ghosts would be doomed.

Its original builder could not afford to finish his replica of a Rhineland castle, so banker Watt Webb took over the ambitious project and completed it. He ordered special furniture and wall hangings on a scale large enough to fit the grandeur of his home. But after 10 years he sold it to buy a more traditional house.

The castle was built on a steep hillside, separated from the road by a lake fed by Rock Creek, which once flowed through the property. Exterior walls were built of native stone, three feet thick. Low stone walls lined the driveway, and a stone carriage house once stood in back.

Because the exterior was a series of towers, all but two of the rooms were circular or oval. The great hall was 20 feet in diameter, encircled by a balcony and topped by a high domed ceiling. On the ground floor, a circular staircase was carved into the wall behind a fireplace, one of six in the house.

The Castle Inn Club, a fashionable place to dine and dance, took over after Webb left. Later the building became a tavern; during Prohibition in the 1920s, it was a base of operation for smugglers supplying liquor to area speakeasies. Later the castle was a convalescent home and a sanitarium.

In 1931 Dr. Joseph Lichtenberg bought the house. The thick stone walls offered a challenge for workmen installing modern plumbing and electricity. In the basement, where the foundation was hewn from the solid rock of the site's limestone cliffs, workmen discovered a hidden passageway to an exit in the cliffs below the house.

The castle was vacant again in the mid-1930s. For a time it was the home of Blevins Davis, producer of the first European touring company of George Gershwin's "Porgy and Bess." A series of residents and several fires have taken their toll on the building. Its ruins are a reminder that maybe there is something in those legends of ghosts.

WEST END HOTEL, 1619 Genessee Street.
Robert Noback, photographer

WEST END HOTEL

Before the railroads came into the city, cattle, principally Texas Longhorns, were driven across the prairie to Kansas City's West Bottoms. (Now the Central Industrial District). Legend has it that the early cattle drovers found Kansas City to be the farthest east cattle could be driven before weight loss significantly reduced the margin of profit. When the railroads made it possible to bring cattle to the West Bottoms in volume, pens were built where the trail-weary cattle were watered and fed for processing and eventual shipment to the lucrative eastern markets.

Short-term living quarters were needed for railroad workers, cowboys, livestock men and others who came in and out of town to profit from the cattle industry. Hotels and boarding houses were built to accommodate the increasing demand.

One of the hotels frequented by these cattlemen was the West End Hotel completed in 1911. It was a small hotel located at 1619 Genessee Street, almost directly across from the Live Stock Exchange. The three-story building with Neoclassical elements, built of red brick and glazed terra cotta, was designed by John W. McKecknie. (McKecknie designed Dr. Herbert G. Tureman's residence in 1910 at 5235 Oak Street, now the Kansas City Miniature Museum and, in 1922, the University Club at 918 Baltimore Avenue.)

As the local cattle market began to fade, related businesses, including the West End Hotel, were forced to hustle for a way to supplement a dwindling income. Several restaurants tried to make a go of it on the first floor of the hotel, but success was fleeting for each.

The hotel building was destroyed in 1982 by a fire. All that remains is a vacant lot.

M any now call the valley below the Quality Hill bluffs, where the Kaw River flows to meet the Missouri River, the Central Industrial District. But as the West Bottoms, it was one of Kansas City's earliest business districts. Before the turn of the century its principal enterprises were the livestock market and meat-packing plants — the first Kansas City industries to reach one million dollars in annual volume.

The first packing plant was not in the West Bottoms at all; it was on the Missouri River levee. It opened in 1859 and operated until the Civil War. In 1867 there were four small packing plants in the West Bottoms, the largest being Plankington & Armour — forerunner of the Armour Packing Company. By the turn of the century, Swift & Company, Wilson & Company, Cudahy Packing Company, and others also were doing business there. This was the only place in the country where all four of the leading meat packing companies had facilities.

But the West Bottoms had more than the meat industry. There were vast rail yards there. Until the Union Station was completed in 1914, the West Bottoms was the city's freight and passenger railway center. By 1900, forty-five major and subsidiary railroads used the Bottoms' Union Depot.

Farmers in horse-drawn wagons went there daily to buy and trade livestock. This attracted seed and farm implement companies, and grain elevators were built to the north. Access to shipping, factories and foundries also made the Bottoms an ideal location for factories.

Kansas City's legendary political dynasty got its start in the West Bottoms. Jim Pendergast arrived in Kansas City in 1876 and found a job working in an iron foundry. He took his winnings from a bet on a horse named "Climax" and invested them in a West Bottoms saloon, naming it

after the horse. Later, he bought a larger saloon and a hotel on St. Louis Avenue near 12th Street, around the corner from the depot. It was referred to as "Pendergast's House." This part of the West Bottoms was compared to New York's rowdy and sordid "Bowery" because of its assortment of saloons, gambling dens, dance halls and brothels. On Ninth Street, near State Line Road, 23 of the 24 buildings were saloons (the block

was called "the wettest block in the world,") and Pendergast's saloon was one of the more reputable places in the area.

Pendergast soon had the reputation of being able to deliver votes to Democratic candidates. He bought a larger saloon at 508 Main Street, near the City Market, but he still held on to his West Bottoms property fighting every effort to clean up the area. He was voted in as First Ward alderman in 1892 and

summoned his three brothers from St. Joseph, Missouri. The youngest, Tom, inherited his brother's contacts and power base when Jim died.

The West Bottoms' colorful history was a mixture of cowboys and cattle barons, gamblers and prostitutes, farmers and immigrants, merchants and speculators, railroaders and politicians, all converging to buy and sell, make and lose fortunes and secure a foothold on the ladder of success.

By 1900 the WEST BOTTOMS was a thriving industrial complex where factories, manufacturing plants, livestock dealers, meat packers and other businesses used the trains and the rivers to transport their merchandise. Kansas City, Missouri Public Library - Missouri Valley Special Collections

The first WESTPORT CITY HALL was built in 1859. This 1896 photo shows the entire Westport police force: Chief of Police Tom Morrison, Ira Emmons and John Conboy. On horseback was the only member of "the mounted brigade": June Collins, a black man. His duty was to round up stray livestock that were held in the city pound and eventually redeemed for a fee. The old City hall was razed in 1897.

Kansas City, Missouri Public Library - Missouri Valley Special Collections

WESTPORT CITY HALL

efore the Civil War the town of West Port (its original name) was better known than the Town of Kansas, referred to as Westport's landing because steamboats dropped off supplies at the levee that were destined for Westport four miles to the south. Westport did not become a part of Kansas City until July 1, 1899.

Westport was the last stop for travelers crossing over into Indian Territory on their way southwest. By 1825 when John McCoy recorded his survey of 10 blocks and named the town, stores there were already doing business with those traveling to the Southwest.

Shops along today's Westport Road and Pennsylvania Avenue sold everything needed to cross the plains: mules, horses, ropes, tents, saddles, flour, guns and other necessities for survival. There were wagon factories, carpentry shops and a candle factory. The

Indian migration, the rush to find gold and the Santa Fe trade made for lucrative business. Westport thrived until the Border Wars and the Civil War promoted the town's decline.

These stores sold their merchandise for cash and there was plenty of money around. The trade attracted every type of man of the West — including Indians who roamed the streets by day and slept in nearby fields at night. Some of Westport's citizens protested that there were far too many people carrying guns in town. It was time for law and order.

In 1859 Westport's City Council, which had been meeting on the second floor of a meat market on the southeast corner of Pennsylvania Avenue and High Street (now 40th Terrace.) decided to build a city hall and jail on that

site. (The "calaboose," as the jail was called, was in the rear of the building.)

In 1895 voters approved bonds to construct a bigger and better city hall costing $15,000 on the old site at Pennsylvania Avenue and High Street. It was also to include a police and fire station. Designed by Frederick E. Hill, the building was of sturdy stone construction with rounded corners and many minarets. On the first floor were the police and fire departments. Upstairs was Mayor D. D. Drake's office, the council chambers, the city court and a dormitory for firemen.

It was finished in 1897. Two years later Westport was absorbed into the City of Kansas City. The building became one of Kansas City's police and fire stations. It was vacated in 1932 and threatened with demolition.

In 1938 the building was purchased by the Campbell-Taggart Company to be used for laboratory research. Sold again in 1945 it was bought by Midwest Research Institute, which would eventually own seven buildings in the vicinity of 40th Street and Pennsylvania Avenue. The old city hall became a chemical engineering center, housing a variety of enterprises including some secret government projects. In 1954 Midwest moved into its new complex on Volker Boulevard. The Steward Sand and Material Company bought the old Westport building for $100,000, proposing to remodel it for offices. However, the building was razed April 18, 1955, erasing the last evidence of Westport's identity as a separate city.

The second WESTPORT CITY HALL was constructed on the same site as the first. Built 1897; demolished in 1955. Today the land is used for a surface parking lot. The Kansas City Star Company

THE ANCIENT VOGEL-WIEDENMANN DWELLING, SEVENTY-TWO YEARS OLD, IS RAZED.

FRED WIEDENMANN'S house at 1303 West 43rd Street (Westport Road and Holly Street). Built in 1857. The house, a showplace in Westport, was torn down in 1924. An empty pizza parlor is on the site.
Kansas City, Missouri Public Library - Missouri Valley Special Collections

Louis Vogel, who came here in the mid-1850s, built his house at Westport and State Line roads. He and the Wiedenmann family owned most of the land surrounding from today's Southwest Trafficway to State Line Road - 39th Street south to Brush Creek Boulevard.
Jackson County Historical Society

FRED WIEDENMANN RESIDENCE

*I*n the mid-1800s, two families owned most of what is today the Volker, West Plaza and Westwood neighborhoods. The Wiedenmann and Vogel farmlands extended from what is now 38th Street to Brush Creek Boulevard and State Line Road to the Southwest Trafficway.

Mary Katherine Wiedenmann emigrated from Germany in 1854 with her seven sons and three daughters. They soon started acquiring land west of the city of Westport. In 1862 the Wiedenmann sons, known to be good carpenters, opened a store in Westport to sell ox yokes and freight wagons for traders on the Santa Fe Trail. The store was on the northwest corner of Westport Road and Pennsylvania Avenue. Later the family made this a grocery store and operated it until 1927. Wiedenmanns still own the building, which now houses Kelly's tavern.

Louis Vogel also arrived in Westport in the mid-1850s with his family. He acquired 200 acres in the area and bought more land as he became prosperous. When Fred Wiedenmann, one of Mary Katherine's sons, married one of Vogel's daughters, Vogel built them a house on the Santa Fe Trail, at 1303 West 43rd Street (now Westport Road.) The house was located near a large fruit orchard and a spring. This made it a natural camping ground for Indians as well as wagonmasters.

The two-story red brick house had a long porch on the south side. Here the family would sit and watch the long wagon trains bound for New Mexico. In 1856 the porch also gave the family a front-row seat at a gun battle. Lawmen killed three bank robbers, running for the Kansas line, in the Wiedenmann's yard. Indians nearby said that the bandits had buried $300,000 in the farm's pasture under a big elm tree, but repeated diggings never found the treasure.

The house was still there after Chestnut Street, now Roanoke Parkway, was cut through the farm. There was some talk about preserving the homestead as a tea house. But it was razed in 1924 to make room for a gasoline station. A two-block street running north from Westport Road, approximately across from where the homestead stood, is named Wiedenmann Street.

WILLIS WOOD THEATER (1902) was on the corner of 11th Street and Baltimore
Avenue. Built in 1902 it was destroyed by fire in 1917.
Kansas City, Missouri Public Library - Missouri Valley Special Collections.

WILLIS WOOD THEATER

*C*olonel Willis Wood had come to Kansas City in the late 1890s from St. Joseph where he had made his money in the wholesale dry-goods trade. When fire destroyed the Coates Opera House on January 1, 1901, Wood decided the city needed a grand theater to replace it.

For the task he hired architect Louis S. Curtiss, who had designed the Baltimore Hotel, across the street from the theater site. Wood lived at the hotel during the construction so he could watch it progress from his window. D. O. Dean, president of the hotel, offered to pay for a tunnel under Baltimore Avenue to connect the buildings (making it easier for theatergoers to visit the hotel's bar between acts.) An auction was held on the theater's opening night, August 25, 1902, for the privilege of being the first to pass through the tunnel. The winning bid was $35.

The classic Beaux-Arts style theater seated 1,527. The main balcony featured "Diamond Horseshoe" seating in the manner of New York's Metropolitan Opera House; seats in the boxes on either side of the proscenium arch sold for the unheard-of price of seven dollars each on opening night. The capacity audience applauded architect Curtiss as he took his box seat.

The stage was large enough to accommodate a treadmill that was considered a technical marvel. During a production of "Ben Hur," two chariots drawn by horses ran a real race on that treadmill.

For three years the Willis Wood was the top theater in town, attracting the best actors, singers and plays. Then, in 1904, the Shubert Theater opened and took the lead. As the audiences grew thinner, the Willis Wood presented plays featuring its stock company of actors, then burlesque, then silent movies.

In 1917 a stock company was again appearing in productions. But barely a week into the new year, an hour after the theater had closed for the night, it caught fire. Flames fed by painted canvas scenery caused the roof to collapse. This created a flue effect, which drew the flames upward in a spectacular blaze that illuminated all of downtown.

The asbestos curtain separating the stage from the seats kept most of the flames backstage. However, damage was so heavy that the theater was declared a total loss and was torn down. The Kansas City Athletic Club was built on the site. Several additions followed, and the building eventually became the Continental Hotel. The Mark Twain Towers now stands on the site.

PSETZLER WINE GARDEN was on the southeast corner of Cleveland and Independence avenues. Natural springs on the property provided water for the wine, and later, for soda pop. A super market is at this location today.
Kansas City, Missouri Public Library - Missouri Valley Special Collections

Frederick Esslinger, an early wine maker, had a wine garden in the Westport area.
Kansas City, Missouri Public Library - Missouri Valley Special Collections

WINE GARDENS

*K*ansas City could hardly be thought of as a winemaking center, but from the late 1870s until after the turn of the century, the area had several small commercial vineyards. They stored their wines in underground cellars and ran wine gardens, where city residents would socialize over glasses of wine.

There were several in the Westport area. Horning's, the oldest, dates back to the 1840s. August Horning's land spread from what is now 38th Street to Westport Road and Main to Holly streets. It was said that his choicest grapes were grown and the best wine was made on Westport Road. Horning kept his wine barrels, along with beer he made from nearby spring water, in natural caves near Holly Street. He dug into the earth and built a domed vault where the temperature never varied. Here he kept his best wine. In 1915, when workmen were excavating the area. they came across the vault — alas, empty.

Frederick Esslinger came to Kansas City in 1850 and opened a watchmaker's store on North Main Street, near the levee. In 1876 he started his wine garden on six acres of land he owned at 39th Street and Belleview Avenue.

People from all over Westport and Kansas City would come in the evenings to sip wine while sitting around tables under the trees. It was a friendly crowd, never rough or drunken.

The Esslingers made their wine from grapes they both grew and purchased. Frederick Esslinger built a house on the southeast corner of 39th Street and Roanoke Road in 1881. He died in 1898, but the wine garden continued until 1904, when the land was sold to be developed for housing. In 1933, when the Esslinger house was razed, workmen found nothing of the well-stocked wine cellar rumored to be under the house.

Peter Muehlebach built his family's wine garden at 41st Street and State Line Road in 1878, on thirty-three acres straddling the state line. The wine garden lasted until 1919, when Prohibition went into effect.

Psetzler Wine Garden on Independence Avenue used natural springs to produce wine from grapes grown on the family's property. The garden lasted until the turn of the century; then the Psetzler family turned the winery into a soda pop factory that made soft drinks that were popular through the 1920s.

Reminiscing about 52 years of being in business, FRED WOLFERMAN marveled how a one-horse and one-clerk grocery store grew into a multi-million dollar a year business. Wolferman died in 1955.
Kansas City, Missouri Public Library - Missouri Valley Special Collections

WOLFERMAN'S STORE at Armour Boulevard and Main Street was constructed on the site of the Thomas H. Mastin residence (1888). Demolished in 1927, the house had been designed by Stanford White.
Wilborn & Associates

The art of grocery display was at its zenith as shown in the WOLFERMAN'S Armour Boulevard and Main Street Store.
Wilborn & Associates

WOLFERMAN'S

"*G*ood things to eat." It's a slogan familiar to Kansas Citians who knew the Wolferman's stores.

German-born Louis Wolferman arrived in Kansas City in 1883; a few years later, he bought a bankrupt grocery store at 317-319 East Ninth Street. His son, Fred, worked as a clerk and drove the delivery wagon pulled by Fannie, a horse, the "third employee." After Fred finished buying produce at the City Market, usually between 4 and 5 a.m., he would stop to pick up hotel orders, then go back to the store. Home and hotel orders were filled, and then daily deliveries began.

Business flourished. Customers liked the personal services that Wolferman offered. He needed more space, and as other businesses edged southward, Wolferman decided to move in 1895 to 1108 Walnut Street. Fourteen years later the building was destroyed by fire. He liked the location, so he put up a new building on the site, designed by the architectural firm of Smith, Rea & Lovitt. It was constructed by George L. Brown & Son. Wolferman's reopened a year after the fire.

The location proved to be an excellent choice. Eleventh and Walnut was a major streetcar transfer point, giving riders the opportunity to shop for groceries.

By this time, Fred was president of the company. His father was vice-president, devoting much of his time to managing their Twin Sycamore Farm at 97th and Holmes streets. (For years, the farm provided most of the store's dairy and poultry products.)

The Walnut Street store expanded to include restaurants — the Grillette, "a few steps down," famous for its Grillette salad dressing, the Balcony, "a few steps up;" the exclusive Tiffin Room on the second floor; and, for quite a while, the Cafeteria on the third floor. Light refreshments were sold in two small Wolferman shops, in the Newman Theater building and at 1116 Main Street. Most of the restaurants were open for breakfast, lunch and dinner, and they also encouraged the after-theater crowd. Daily waiting lines attested to their popularity. When customers were finished eating, they could, on their way out, buy many of their favorite items, such as the famous hermit cookies, English muffins, salad dressings and homemade candies.

Wolferman stressed personal and courteous service. Quality in everything became a trademark: "We only buy what we cannot make better." A branch at 3943 Main Street became too small and rather than enlarge it, Fred Wolferman decided to build a new store at 9 - 15 West Armour Boulevard. That store, a radical departure from the traditional concept of a grocery store, opened on October 7, 1937.

Edward W. Tanner, who for many years was associated with the J. C. Nichols Company, designed the Armour Boulevard store in the shape of a Maltese cross. It was built by the Long Construction Company of monolithic concrete. Structural glass

panels ran from above the doorways to the service areas in back. Entrances were at the two front corners.

The high-domed central room had an elevated platform where telephone order clerks worked. Each of the four wings off the center housed a specialty department: dairy products and the delicatessen, bakery goods, fruits and vegetables, and meats. Much of the building was off-limits to customers as it was used for assembling orders, refrigeration and storerooms. The equipment alone was installed at a cost of $50,000, half the cost of the building.

The building sat back some 20 feet from the sidewalk and had small display windows, rather than the usual large ones in a building whose main entrance was off the sidewalk.

Beginning in 1925, Frances Royster Williams, the creator of the

children's feature "Cuddles and Tuckie," in *The Kansas City Times* was responsible for Wolferman's advertisements. Her designs could be found on butter and egg cartons, salad dressings, liquor bottle labels, and the clever menu covers. Wolferman's sponsored the radio version of "Cuddles and Tuckie" for 10 years.

During the Second World War, rationing of some cooking ingredients limited product selections, and gasoline shortages also affected business, particularly the branch stores. In the 1950s, Kansas City began turning its back on public transportation. That and the exodus southward provided sufficient reason to close the downtown store in 1972. The building was demolished the same year. The growth of chain groceries and suburban living contributed to the demise of the Armour Boulevard store. It was demolished and the site became parking for the American Bank.

From a December 3, 1934 advertisement in The Kansas City Times: *The Grillette, special Plate Luncheon cost all of 40 cents in the WOLFERMAN'S STORE, 1108 Walnut Street.*
Kansas City Museum - Kansas City, Missouri

YACHT CLUB on the Blue River at 15th Street was built in 1908.
Kansas City, Missouri Parks and Recreation Department

YACHT CLUB

A Yacht Club on the Blue River? Yes, in 1908 The Kansas City Yacht Club was organized and by the next year a clubhouse was built on the Blue River bank at 15th Street. About 100 club members docked their boats at the club: canoes, rowboats and motor boats. People even lived nearby on houseboats. The Paddle and Camp club located up stream held competitive regattas with the Yacht Club each spring.

Although George E. Kessler, architect for the Kansas City Parks and Boulevard system, had a dream of beautifying the Blue River, it was never accomplished. The river is known today mainly for its flooding. Even though there has been repeated diversion of its waters by dams and through large underground sewer pipes, the river still floods almost yearly in the low lands east of Brush Creek and north into the city's Blue Valley district. The force of the destruction of the Blue River was felt in the September 12th, 1977 flood and again in the spring flood of 1990.

When the first white man arrived in the area he found Indian trails through the forest leading to and from the Blue River. The trappers, settlers and Santa Fe traders followed these same trails to move from Independence west to the Town of Kansas and Westport. During the Civil War, Confederate troops advancing on Kansas City battled their way across the Blue River.

The Blue River flows from Wolf Creek in Johnson County, Kansas. Ten streams feed into its 50-mile route. The river enters Kansas City west of Holmes Street about a half mile south of Martin City, Missouri, then flows northeastward toward the Missouri River.

In the 1880s covered bridges spanned the river. There was one on a road connecting Independence with the area near the Sheffield Steel mills (now ARMCO Steel.) It was destroyed by an 1886 cyclone. Another bridge is remembered by name. It was built in the late 1880s on the Bryce B. Smith farm near 110th Street. It was a tin bridge painted red and gave the residential district in that area the name "Red Bridge."

*JOHN GEORGE BRAECKLEIN. This
sketch is from AS WE SEE THEM, a book
by artist "Artigue."*
Kansas City, Missouri Public Library -
Missouri Valley Special Collections

JOHN GEORGE BRAECKLEIN (1865-1958)

Braecklein, at the age of 23, designed the Heist Building (1888) at 724 Main Street. He was one of the original 125 members of Epperson Megaphone Minstrel Company.

OCTAVE CHANUTE (1832-1910)

Born in Paris, the "roly-poly Frenchman" became a nationally recognized civil engineer and a pioneer aviation enthusiast. For two years he was the city engineer for Kansas City, Missouri, serving in the same capacity for various railroad companies. Kansas City's original stockyards, established in 1870, were designed by Chanute, as were the Chicago Stockyards. Of tremendous interest to him was the prospect of flying. He worked with gliders, was an advisor and friend of the Wright Brothers and was frequently present at their experiments.

ASA BEEBE CROSS (1826-1894)

Acknowledged as Kansas City's first professional architect. Cross moved to Kansas City from St. Louis in 1858, and began what has been regarded as an architectural dynasty, perpetuated through his son-in-law, Alfred E. Barnes, a partner in the firm Hoit, Price & Barnes. Buildings designed by Cross include St. Patrick's Church and Rectory (1874-75) at 800 Cherry Street (the Rectory has been demolished); the Vaile Mansion (1881) at 1550 North Liberty Street, Independence and the Exchange Building (1877), 502 Delaware Street.

OCTAVE CHANUTE.
Kansas City, Missouri Public Library -
Missouri Valley Special Collections

LOUIS SINGLETON CURTISS (1865-1924)

The Canadian-born architect arrived in Kansas City sometime before 1890, claiming previous training at the L'Ecole des Beaux Arts in Paris. (Such attendance is not noted in the school's records.) Some believe Curtiss came to Kansas City aware of the building boom that was taking place. Whether formally trained or not he left an architectural legacy. It included the Folly Theater (1900) at 300 West 12th Street; the Bernard Corrigan residence (1912-1913) at 1200 West 55th Street and his own apartment and office (1908-1909) at 1118 McGee Street. Just a tad over 5 feet 6 inches tall, a confirmed bachelor, Curtiss owned a single-seat Winston, one of Kansas City's first automobiles. He died June 24, 1924 and is buried in an unmarked grave in Mount Washington Cemetery.

LOUIS SINGLETON CURTISS

GREENBAUM, HARDY & SCHUMACHER

Samuel Greenbaum was born in 1886 in Topeka, Kansas.
Arthur Raymond Hardy (1885-1966)
Ramon Schumacher, Sr. died 1975.
Schumacher's design for the Liberty Memorial competition placed third. Two buildings that were principally his design are the Linwood Boulevard Presbyterian Church and the old Law School building on the University of Missouri - Kansas City campus. Buildings designed by the firm include Oakwood Country Club (1912) and Keneseth Israel-Beth Shalom Synagogue (1926-1927) at 3400 The Paseo.

FREDERIC E. HILL

He was born in Minnesota and educated at the University of Minnesota. From 1880-1881 he was a special student in architecture at the Massachusetts Institute of Technology and later joined the prestigious New York firm of McKim, Mead & White. He died in 1923.

JAMES OLIVER HOGG (about 1858- 1941)

Before 1900, Hogg formed a partnership with W. W. Rose, an architect who later became mayor of Kansas City, Kansas. Together they designed many Kansas City, Kansas school buildings. Hogg was responsible for the design of several buildings on the Park College campus.

HORACE LA PIERRE (1873-1945)

A genius with a brush, LaPierre's true love was art but, unfortunately, it did not provide a living. Described through the years as growing more "five-by-five-ish" he would accept a design commission to support his life as an artist. An epicurean, LaPierre was well known in most of the downtown eating establishments. Those who were prepared to have him design a house did it with the understanding they must be unduly patient for he was an extremely slow worker. But the wait was worth it as seen in the "extraordinary" house built in 1924 for George H. Wright at 5940 Ward Parkway. It took over three years to complete.

JESSE LAUCH (d. 1969)

Lauch was the architect for several apartment buildings that are located on the western edge of the Country Club Plaza, the Hotel Phillips (106 West 12th Street), and while a member of the architectural firm of Boillot & Lauch, The Walnuts at 5049 Wornall Road.

JOHN W. MCKECKNIE (1862-1934)

JOHN W. McKECKNIE.
Kansas City, Missouri Public Library -
Missouri Valley Special Collections

Born in Clarksville, Ohio, he was graduated from Princeton University in 1886 and continued his education in architecture at the Columbia School of Mines in New York City. In 1898 he moved to Kansas City and for two years worked for Hucke & Sexton Contracting and Building Company. For the next 14 years he practiced alone until he formed a partnership with Frank E. Trask, a graduate of New York's Columbia School of Architecture. Among the buildings he designed are the Gumbel Building (1903-1904) at 801 Walnut Street, the Siegrist Engraving Company Building (1911-1912) at 924 Oak Street, the Calvin Hunt residence (1904) at 3616 Gladstone Boulevard and the James F. Halpin residence (1913) at 1226 West 56th Street.

NELLE E. PETERS (1884-1974)

Born in Niagara, North Dakota as Nelle Nichols, she attended Buena Vista College in Storm Lake, Iowa. Although there is no record that she had any formal training in architecture, she found drawing mechanical things very appealing. "Architecture is a mathematical problem," said Peters, and she loved such a problem.

Around 1909 Nichols came to Kansas City joining an office managed by Ernest O. Brostrom, a practicing architect. She married but after a number of years, divorced. She practiced on her own but finally joined forces with Charles E. Phillips, founder of the Phillips Building Company. To Peters' credit are literally hundreds of apartment buildings, many in the Country Club Plaza area, such as the James Russell Lowell Apartments (1927-1929) at 722 Ward Parkway and a group of English-style buildings in the 700 block of West 48th Street. She designed the Luzier Cosmetic Company building (1928) at 3216 Gillham Plaza. Peters, who was always noted on the city's building permits as N. E. Peters, disguised her gender. She was a true phenomenon in what was a male-dominated profession.

NELLE E. PETERS.

ROOT & SIEMENS

Walter Clark Root (1859-1925) was born in Atlanta, Georgia. He came to Kansas City in 1886, where he married Lorne Bullene, daughter of Thomas B. Bullene who was an early partner in what was to become Emery, Bird, Thayer Dry-Goods Company. In 1896 Root formed a partnership with George Mellin Siemens.

The firm of Root & Siemens made a considerable contribution to Kansas City's built environment. Of particular note are the Scarritt Building (1906-1907) 818 Grand Avenue, the Scarritt Arcade (1906-1907) 819 Walnut Street, the Country Club Congregational Church (1925-1926; addition 1948) at 205 West 65th Street and the Penn Valley Park Maintenance Building (1900-1910) at 3001 Central Street.

WALTER CLARK ROOT. This sketch is from AS WE SEE THEM, a book by artist "Artigue."
Kansas City, Missouri Public Library -
Missouri Valley Special Collections

CHARLES E. SHEPARD (about 1868 - 1932)

Shepard was born in Stuart, Iowa. He graduated from the University of Iowa and came to Kansas City where he formed a partnership with

Ernest H. Farrar. It lasted until 1910, when Farrar retired. The next year Albert Wiser joined the firm which became known as Shepard, Farrar & Wiser.

Shepard was instrumental in the design of the Georgian Court Apartments (1917) at 400 East Armour Boulevard, the Arthur P. Tureman residence (1912-1917) 618 Brush Creek Boulevard, a Prairie School type residence (1915) at 5225 Wyandotte Street and a house (1911) at 3601 Charlotte Street.

CHARLES A. SMITH (1867-1948)

Smith moved to Kansas City from Des Moines in 1887 and formed a partnership with William F. Hackney, an architect who had also just arrived in the city. Smith was appointed in 1898 as the architect to the Kansas City School District, a position he held until 1936. He designed over 50 school buildings before his retirement.

During that time he was an active partner in the architectural firm of Smith, Rea & Lovitt, which was dissolved in 1920. One of the buildings designed by them with George E. McIntyre, was the Firestone Building (1915) at 2001 Grand Avenue. Smith designed the Professional Building (completed in 1930) at 1103 Grand Avenue where he maintained his office.

EDWARD W. TANNER (1895-1974)

Born in Cottonwood, Kansas, Tanner was a member of the first graduating class of the University of Kansas School of Architecture. From 1919 to 1964 he served as the principal designer for the J. C. Nichols Company. He designed dozens of homes in the Country Club District and in Mission Hills, Kansas, as well as a number of shopping centers. One of his most frequently cited houses is the Walter Edwin Bixby residence (1935-37) at 6505 State Line Road. In the commercial field he will be remembered for his part (along with Edward Buehler Delk), in creating the Country Club Plaza. Begun in 1922, it remains one of the city's premier shopping centers. Tanner also designed the small group of shops at 50th Street and State Line Road, the Crestwood Shops (1922) on the south side of 55th Street between Oak Street and Brookside Boulevard, and in 1948 the Prairie Village Shopping Center at 69th Street and Mission Road. Not designed in a traditional style is the "streamline modern" residence at 5622 Chadwick Street, Fairway, Kansas, and the Kansas City, Missouri Public Library and Board of Education Building (1959) at 311 East 12th Street.

ADRIANCE VAN BRUNT (1836-1913)

Born in New Jersey, Van Brunt moved to Kansas City in 1878 and in the early 1880s formed the firm of A. Van Brunt & Company. In 1892 Mayor Ben Holmes appointed Van Brunt to the Kansas City Park Board. Adriance and his brother, John (with whom he had formed a partnership) designed residences at 810 W. 52nd Street (1910) and at 5208 Belleview Avenue.

HENRY VAN BRUNT (1832-1903)

Born in Boston, Massachusetts, Van Brunt attended Boston Latin School and graduated from Harvard University. He moved to Kansas City in 1885 and formed a partnership with Frank Howe, one of the city's earliest architectural partnerships. At the time, it was the leading architectural firm west of the Mississippi River. Together they designed a number of Kansas City's well-known buildings — the Blossom House (1888) at 1032 Pennsylvania Avenue, the August R. Meyer Residence (1896-1897; addition 1929) at 4415 Warwick Boulevard and the Coates House Hotel, (south wing, 1886-1887; north wing, 1898-1901) at 1005 Broadway.

STANFORD WHITE (1853-1906)

Born in New York City, White in 1874 joined the office of famed architect H. H. Richardson of Boston, Massachusetts. Six years later he became a partner in the firm of McKim, Mead & White. Much of the decorative detail of New York City's Villard Houses and Madison Square Garden was of his design. Adapting the architecture of the French Chateau, White designed in 1888, a residence on the southwest corner of Armour Boulevard and Main Street for Thomas H. Mastin.

WILDER & WIGHT

Edward T. Wilder was born in Topeka, Kansas. He attended Cornell University and later became associated with the most prestigious New York City architectural firm of McKim, Mead & White. He retired from practice in 1912.

Thomas Wight (1874-1949) came to Kansas City from New York City in 1904, having worked in the McKim, Mead & White office. He was said to have had a special preference for "ecclesiastical monumental design" as seen in his design of the Grace and Holy Trinity Cathedral tower (1938) 415 West 13th Street. The firm was responsible for designing the First National Bank Building (1904-1906) 14 West 10th Street, the Edwin Shields residence (1909) 5110 Cherry Street, now part of the University of Missouri-Kansas City; and the Thomas H. Swope Memorial and Mausoleum (1916-1917) in Swope Park.

ACKNOWLEDGEMENTS

M any individuals and organizations have contributed information and photographs to this book. We wish to acknowledge the following: Denise Morrison of the Kansas City Museum, George L. Eib of the Kansas City, Missouri Parks and Recreation Department; *The Kansas City Star*; David Boutros of the Western Missouri Historical Manuscript Collection - Kansas City, Missouri; The Native Sons of Greater Kansas City; Kathleen Halcro and Matthew Veatch of The Jackson County Historical Society; Peggy Smith of The Westport Historical Society; Kate Kern and Lisa Lassman Briscoe of the Landmarks Commission of Kansas City, Missouri, Wally Emerson, and Douglas Hudson.

We also are indebted to the following who delved into their memories and material providing us with stories and valuable photographs: Mary Keck, Mrs. Landon Laird, Jean Sanderson, Herb Simon, Frances DeAngelo, Marie Chambers, Patty Ducoulombier, Betty Hodges, Sister Corine Joyce, Sister Zita Marie Bruns, Chris Wilborn, Jim Murray, Wilda Sandy, John Robert Flynn, Barbara F. Wynn, LaVierge Kaiser, Jerry P. Fogel, Kevin Anderson, Aurora Davis, Frances Royster Williams, Stephanie Wolff, Mary Louise Hinton, Mrs. Lillian Orme, Mrs. James Street, Irene Marcus, Norma Webster, Virginia Goodman, Anne O'Hare, Mrs. Bayard Grant, John Lewin, Sherry Piland, J. Glen Travis, Frank J. Adler, Terry Egelhoff, Joan Jordan, Mary Eaton, and Dr. George Ehrlich.

Our special appreciation goes to the staff of the Kansas City, Missouri Public Library's Missouri Valley Special Collections: Gloria Maxwell, Department Head; Marjorie Kinney, Sara Hallier, Sandra Gates, Beth Whitaker, Kathryn Maciel, Alberta Francisko, Loman Cansler, Deonna Ard and Johnetta King. Without their aid and support this book would not have been possible.

ABOUT THE AUTHORS

Dory DeAngelo has written extensively about Kansas City history. She has had published over 150 articles in newspapers and magazines and has written three books: "Voices Across Time", "The Plaza, Kansas City's World Famous Shopping Center", and "Passages Through Time, Stories About Kansas City, Missouri and its Northeast Neighborhood". She coordinated the publication of the Kansas City Landmarks Commission "A Place in Time".

Dory does historic research for many individuals, companies and authors, screen and television writers from across the country. She majored in theater at the University of Missouri-Kansas City and worked for The Starlight Theater, Missouri Repertory Theater and the Lyric Opera. Her father, Pete DeAngelo, was a musician who performed at Electric Park and various vaudeville theaters. His stories about the city's theaters during the first quarter of this century got Dory interested in history.

Jane Fifield Flynn, a native Kansas Citian, has long been associated with history and preservations efforts in the community. From 1976 to mid-1987 she was the administrator of the Landmarks Commission of Kansas City, Missouri. She has more than a dozen professional affiliations in her field of interest including Historic Kansas City Foundation, Preservation Action, and the National Trust for Historic Preservation. Presently she is serving her second term as the president of the Jackson County Historical Society. In 1990, Governor John Ashcroft appointed her a member of the Missouri Advisory Council on Historic Preservation. She is also a member of the Forty Years Ago Column Club. Her family roots run deep, and an alert reader of this volume will note on page 83 the reference to Rev. James W. Fifield, pastor of the First Congregational Church (1902-04), her grandfather.

Mrs. Flynn recently completed *Kansas City Women of Independent Minds*: a book relating the personal history of some women who had a meaningful association with Kansas City.

OLD AMERICAN ROYAL

F or over 70 years livestock and equine aristocracy moved along the tanbark on their way to judgement day. It was in the fall of the year, and the American Royal Live Stock and Horse Show was underway.

With a rapidly growing Kansas City cattle market, (By 1871 over 700,000 head of cattle were processed through the stockyards.) competition on best of breeds and within breeds had become common practice. In 1889 the National Hereford Show was held, for an official judging, in a tent on the stockyard's grounds. A year later Shorthorn breeders joined the show. So many persons attended that some had to be turned away. For ten years the show lacked a permanent home, and this posed quite a problem because more breeds of cattle, sheep, swine, poultry, and horses were entered. In 1909, with an influx of out-state competitors, the show was held in the old Convention Hall, and in 1917 and 1918 it was moved to Electric Park at 46th Street and The Paseo. In 1919 it returned to Convention Hall.

A permanent building was essential. In November 1922, a two-story building, covering six acres, was dedicated. Designed by Charles E. Smith (St. Louis), the cost of construction was $650,000. With the Kansas City Chamber of Commerce and three livestock breeders leading the way by raising $100,000, the Kansas City Stock Yards Company made up the difference. The Lindsborg chorus sang music from the "Messiah." Speeches were made by the governors of Missouri and Kansas.

The building was heavily damaged in a fire during the 1926 Automobile Show which cost the life of Captain John Crane of the fire department. On Friday, July 13, 1951, the Kaw River flooded out its banks extensively damaging much of the stockyards and part of the American Royal Building. With strong urgings from city officials, the building was repaired in time for the fall show.

Demolition of the "grand old building" began in December 1991.

The main entrance of the American Royal Arena located at 23rd and Wyoming streets.
Landmarks Commission of Kansas City, Missouri

GENERAL HOSPITAL

ocated high on a hill at 2315 Locust Street, the building was completed in 1908, as the city's first charitable hospital providing medical services for the indigent. It also served as a teaching hospital. Reflecting Jacobean stylistic elements, it was designed by prominent local architects Frederick C. Gunn, Walter C. Root, and George Siemens. Four and one-half acres of land had in 1905, been donated for the hospital by Colonel Thomas Hunton Swope. Over the years there were seven additions to the building.

On April 13, 1991, the original (north) section was demolished for Children's Mercy Hospital expanded parking. The other sections had been demolished earlier despite attempts by the Friends of General Hospital to seek a plan for the use of the building.

On the left is the north wing of General Hospital, the last section to be demolished.
Landmarks Commission of Kansas City, Missouri

THE LYKINS HOUSE

*U*pon its completion in 1857, this Classic-Revival house was considered the handsomest house west of St. Louis. Dr. Johnston A. Lykins, the first official mayor of Kansas City and the founder and first president of the Mechanics Bank, built it for his second wife, Martha. No expense was spared. Most of the construction materials came by steamboat from the East. The wood used throughout the home was from Ohio. All at a cost of $20,000. The clay for the bricks came from the banks of the Missouri River.

Originally located near the southeast corner of 12th and Washington streets, it was moved across the street in 1889. Over six additions occurred between 1889 and 1938. The building endured a variety of uses including that of a hotel housing the ladies of the night. When the last owner's redevelopment plans failed, the building was left roofless and windowless, completely exposed to nature's capriciousness. The building was demolished in 1990.

The Dr. Johnston A. Lykins Residence,
1204 Washington Street, as it appeared
with all of its many additions.
Landmarks Commission of Kansas
City, Missouri

PASEO HIGH SCHOOL

I t was an imposing sight, standing high on a hill overlooking The Paseo at 47th Street. When the doors opened on September 26, 1926, it was considered by the Kansas City Board of Education as the "flagship," the ultimate in secondary education technology and equipment.

Designed by Charles A. Smith, the school board's architect for more than 38 years, it was constructed of reinforced frame concrete and clad in limestone quarried at the site. It was the only public school building of Collegiate Gothic style and one of three constructed of native stone.

The school building boasted the Paseo Branch of the public library, 35 classrooms, and domestic science rooms. Later additions included an auditorium and an indoor swimming pool along with doubling the number of classrooms. Sixty-four years later, a victim of court-ordered desegregation plan, the building was deemed outmoded and obsolete. Legal actions by the Friends of Paseo High School, which had been formed to save the building, failed. On November 29, 1990, by implosion, the building was demolished. When the dust settled, much of the front facade, including the main tower, remained standing, having defied the power of the explosives.

Paseo High School as it stood high on the hill overlooking 47th Street and The Paseo.
Landmarks Commission of Kansas City, Missouri

KANSAS CITY STOCKYARDS

With a rapidly growing, "hungry" Eastern market, great numbers of Arkansas and Texas cattle were, by the late 1860s being driven to an area east of the Kaw River and just south of the Missouri River, known as the West Bottoms. In 1867, with the coming of the railroads into the area, over 35,000 cattle were unloaded for rest, feed, and water into temporary fenced enclosures. A year later the number doubled. Anticipating further increases, in 1870 Colonel L.V. Morse, superintendent of the Hannibal & St. Joseph Railroad, and James W. Joy constructed 11 pens, 15 unloading chutes, and a pair of Fairbanks scales. Soon afterwards some 100,000 head of cattle were processed through the yards.

In 1871 the first livestock exchange building was constructed and the Kansas Stock Yards was reorganized and became known as the Kansas City Stock Yards. The next year on about 5.5 acres new pens, railroad docks, a barn, sheds for horses and mules and a race track with a covered amphitheater were constructed. By 1872 hogs had become a lucrative market, as had sheep by 1876. Pens were constructed for them.

By the early 1950s the local cattle market dwindled resulting in a reduction in meat processing at packing plants such as Armour and Cudhay. It was not long before disuse and neglect took a toll. Anticipating other uses for the land, pens, chutes and loading docks were gradually removed. Today few elements remain that give any sense of the role the livestock industry played in the economic growth of Kansas City.

Kansas City Stockyards on a busy market day.
Kansas City, Missouri
Public Library-Missouri
Valley Special Collections

1200 BLOCK OF PENNSYLVANIA AVENUE

W ith its natural scenic beauty and view of the Kaw and Missouri rivers, Quality Hill beginning after the Civil War was for over 30 years one of the most prestigious neighborhoods in the city. It included structures in the 1200 block of Pennsylvania Avenue, which represented several architectural styles: Queen Anne, Neo-Romanesque, "Builder's Vernacular," and Italianate Revival. The buildings were constructed and occupied by some of the city's leading citizens.

The earliest single-family dwelling was at 1240 Pennsylvania Avenue and was built for the Reverend C.J. Hatterus. In 1877 a double townhouse located at 1228-30 was constructed, followed ten years later by another one at 1232-34 Pennsylvania Avenue.

The decline of Quality Hill began shortly after the turn-of-the-century. There were the offensive odors blowing in from the stockyards and meatpacking plants situated in the West Bottoms, and lots were filled leaving no space for new construction. Families moved south, building houses in Hyde Park, Roanoke, and along Armour Boulevard.

Over a period of time the once-elegant homes were divided for multi-family use. Some became rooming houses, apartment houses and missions; others were just abandoned. Unsuccessful attempts to finance rehabilitation of the houses, questionable fires, and ownership neglect exacted a terrible toll.

A small sample of the houses that graced the 1200 block of Pennsylvania Avenue.
Landmarks Commission of Kansas City, Missouri